Cambridge School
Shakespeare

Much Ado About Nothing

Edited by Mary Berry and Michael Clamp

Series Editor: Rex Gibson
Director, Shakespeare and Schools Project

CAMBRIDGE
UNIVERSITY PRESS

CAMBRIDGE UNIVERSITY PRESS
Cambridge, New York, Melbourne, Madrid, Cape Town,
Singapore, São Paulo, Delhi, Mexico City

Cambridge University Press
The Edinburgh Building, Cambridge CB2 8RU, UK

www.cambridge.org
Information on this title: www.cambridge.org/9780521618724

First published 1993
Second edition 2005
10th printing 2012

Printed in the United Kingdom at the University Press, Cambridge

A catalogue record for this publication is available from the British Library

ISBN 978-0-521-61872-4 Paperback

ACKNOWLEDGEMENTS
Thanks are due to the following for permission to reproduce illustrations:
Cover, v, vii, viii, ix, x, xi, 22, 58, 62, 74, 82, 98, 132, 142, 154, 163, 177, 178, 179, 180, 191*t*,
193, 194*t*, Donald Cooper/Photostage; vi, Sam Goldwyn/Renaissance Films/BBC/The
Kobal Collection/Coote, Clive; xii*t*, Sam Goldwyn/Renaissance Films/BBC/The Kobal
Collection; xii*b*, 169, Zoë Dominic; 2, 6, 25, 92, 110, 118, 150, Ivan Kyncl; 32, 96, 108,
126, 175*t*, Chris Davies; 46, 80, 102, 175*b*, Joe Cocks Studio Collection © Shakespeare
Birthplace Trust; 54, Stuart Morris; 88, printed by kind permission of The Trustees
of the Cowdray Settled Estate, photograph Photographic Survey, Courtauld Institute of
Art; 171, private collection, on loan to the National Portrait Gallery, London; 173, with
the kind permission of The Viscount Daventry; 190, 191*b*, John Tramper; 192, V & A
Images; 194*b*, photographer Reg Wilson © Royal Shakespeare Company.

Cover design by Smith

Contents

Cambridge School
Shakespeare

This edition of *Much Ado About Nothing* is part of the **Cambridge School Shakespeare** series. Like every other play in the series, it has been specially prepared to help all students in schools and colleges.

This *Much Ado About Nothing* aims to be different from other editions of the play. It invites you to bring the play to life in your classroom, hall or drama studio through enjoyable activities that will increase your understanding. Actors have created their different interpretations of the play over the centuries. Similarly, you are encouraged to make up your own mind about *Much Ado About Nothing*, rather than having someone else's interpretation handed down to you.

Cambridge School Shakespeare does not offer you a cut-down or simplified version of the play. This is Shakespeare's language, filled with imaginative possibilities. You will find on every left-hand page: a summary of the action, an explanation of unfamiliar words, a choice of activities on Shakespeare's language, characters and stories.

Between each act and in the pages at the end of the play, you will find notes, illustrations and activities. These will help to increase your understanding of the whole play.

There are a large number of activities to give you the widest choice to suit your own particular needs. Please don't think you have to do every one. Choose the activities that will help you most.

This edition will be of value to you whether you are studying for an examination, reading for pleasure, or thinking of putting on the play to entertain others. You can work on the activities on your own or in groups. Many of the activities suggest a particular group size, but don't be afraid to make up larger or smaller groups to suit your own purposes.

Although you are invited to treat *Much Ado About Nothing* as a play, you don't need special dramatic or theatrical skills to do the activities. By choosing your activities, and by exploring and experimenting, you can make your own interpretations of Shakespeare's language, characters and stories. Whatever you do, remember that Shakespeare wrote his plays to be acted, watched and enjoyed.

Rex Gibson

This edition of *Much Ado About Nothing* uses the text of the play established by F. H. Mares in **The New Cambridge Shakespeare**.

The warring couple

'I wonder that you will still be talking, Signor Benedick, nobody marks you.' *Much Ado About Nothing* is particularly admired for the wit and intelligence of Beatrice and Benedick, the warring couple comically tricked into falling in love.

The soldiers return

The story begins with the arrival of Don Pedro's army. In this 1993 Branagh film, the young women of Governor Leonato's household, led by Beatrice (left) and Leonato's daughter Hero (centre), scamper excitedly down the hill to greet the prince's men.

Don Pedro's company enters Governor Leonato's courtyard. The prince (centre) has Count Claudio and Signor Benedick on his right. On the prince's left is his brother Don John, the defeated leader of the recent rebellion.

The young war hero and the governor's daughter

Count Claudio, highly praised for his bravery in the recent war, wishes to marry Hero, Leonato's only child. The wealthy governor of Messina is only too delighted to have his daughter make such a magnificent alliance.

'In mine eye, she is the sweetest lady that ever I looked on.' Below, Hero with her father.

Deception and disguise

Don Pedro plans to help Claudio win Hero's heart. At the masked ball he poses as his young friend, woos Hero and gains her consent to marry.

'She told me, not thinking I had been myself, that I was the prince's jester.' At the masked ball, Benedick also pretends to be someone else. Beatrice, however, sees through his disguise and uses the opportunity to make wittily insulting comments about the 'absent Benedick'.

Tricked into love

Don Pedro arranges a second deception. Benedick and Beatrice are both tricked into believing the other is secretly in love with them. Benedick's overhearing of his friends' 'secret' conversation is often played for laughs, as in this production above, set in twentieth-century Sicily.

The 'gulling' (tricking) of Beatrice is usually played more seriously. The mirror she hides behind here is made of semi-transparent glass, so the audience can see both the hoaxers and Beatrice's shocked yet delighted reaction.

Angry accusations

Don John maliciously tricks Claudio and Don Pedro into believing they have seen Hero entertaining another man in her bedroom. At the wedding ceremony, Claudio publicly and savagely rejects Hero as nothing but a common whore.

Faced with such accusations, Hero faints with shock. Beatrice believes her cousin to be innocent. She urges Benedick to challenge Claudio to single combat. On the Friar's advice, Leonato orders that Hero be hidden and reported dead until her innocence is proved.

Saved by the clowns

Fortunately, Don John's plot is accidentally uncovered by the town's incompetent Watchmen, led by Dogberry (second left), their even more inept Master Constable. Still believing Hero is dead, a penitent Claudio agrees to marry Leonato's niece, said to be the 'image' of Hero. She is, of course, Hero herself.

When love sonnets in their own handwriting are produced, Beatrice and Benedick reluctantly admit their love for each other and also agree to marry.

'Let's have a dance ere we are married'

A delighted Benedick kisses his bride-to-be, then leads the whole company in a celebratory dance. Not even news that Don John has been captured can spoil his happiness.

'Prince, thou art sad, get thee a wife, get thee a wife'. Productions often show Don Pedro (seated, left) alone at the end of the play, while couples dance happily around him.

List of characters

Leonato's Household

SIGNOR LEONATO governor of Messina
SIGNOR ANTONIO his brother
HERO Leonato's only daughter
BEATRICE an orphan, Leonato's niece
MARGARET ⎫
URSULA ⎬ gentlewomen attending on Hero
FRIAR FRANCIS
Musicians, Attendants, Maskers and Wedding Guests

The Military

DON PEDRO Prince of Arragon
DON JOHN his bastard brother
COUNT CLAUDIO of Florence ⎫
SIGNOR BENEDICK of Padua ⎬ companions of Don Pedro
BORACHIO ⎫
CONRADE ⎬ followers of Don John
MESSENGER
BALTHASAR a singer
BOY servant to Benedick

The Town

DOGBERRY Constable of Messina
VERGES Deputy Constable (or Headborough)
SEXTON
GEORGE SEACOAL Senior Watchman
WATCHMAN 1
WATCHMAN 2
Other Watchmen

The play is set in Messina, Sicily

A Messenger brings a letter informing Governor Leonato that Don Pedro and his victorious army will shortly arrive in Messina. The Messenger reports that young Count Claudio has performed great deeds of bravery in the war.

A hit! A hit! Beatrice fences with her uncle, Leonato.

1 Powerful men, powerless women? (in groups of about seven)

The 1990 Royal Shakespeare Company production highlighted this as a major theme of the play by having the lights come up to reveal Beatrice defeating her uncle in a fencing bout, much to the delight of the women watching.

Sit in a circle and read through lines 1–118. What clues can you find in the way characters talk and behave to suggest that this play will be very much concerned with the position of women in a male-dominated world? Find the words Leonato uses to describe Beatrice and Benedick's 'battle of the sexes'.

by this by now	**equally remembered** suitably rewarded
three leagues about nine miles	
gentlemen noblemen	**figure** appearance
action battle	**bettered expectation** surpassed all expectations
sort high rank, nobility	
none of name no one well known	**badge** show or sign
achiever winner	**kind** natural

Much Ado About Nothing

Act 1 Scene 1
Messina Leonato's house

Enter LEONATO, governor of Messina, HERO his daughter and
BEATRICE his niece, with a MESSENGER

LEONATO I learn in this letter, that Don Pedro of Arragon comes this
night to Messina.

MESSENGER He is very near by this, he was not three leagues off when I
left him.

LEONATO How many gentlemen have you lost in this action?   5

MESSENGER But few of any sort, and none of name.

LEONATO A victory is twice itself, when the achiever brings home full
numbers. I find here, that Don Pedro hath bestowed much honour on
a young Florentine called Claudio.

MESSENGER Much deserved on his part, and equally remembered by   10
Don Pedro. He hath borne himself beyond the promise of his age,
doing in the figure of a lamb the feats of a lion. He hath indeed better
bettered expectation than you must expect of me to tell you how.

LEONATO He hath an uncle here in Messina will be very much glad of it.

MESSENGER I have already delivered him letters, and there appears   15
much joy in him, even so much that joy could not show itself modest
enough without a badge of bitterness.

LEONATO Did he break out into tears?

MESSENGER In great measure.

LEONATO A kind overflow of kindness: there are no faces truer than   20
those that are so washed. How much better is it to weep at joy, than to
joy at weeping!

Beatrice questions the Messenger about Benedick, sarcastically calling him Signor Mountanto. Faced with a barrage of mocking comments about a fellow soldier, the Messenger politely attempts to defend Benedick's reputation.

1 Show how elegantly the men speak (in pairs)

Read aloud several times the opening conversation between Leonato and the Messenger (lines 1–22). Practise speaking with supreme self-confidence. Gesture or mime to emphasise balances and contrasts (e.g. 'Much deserved' is balanced with 'equally remembered'). Listen for and stress the sound patterns made by alliteration (repeated initial consonants), or different forms of the same word (e.g. 'better bettered').

2 Beatrice – a formidable woman (in groups of about six)

Everything Beatrice says in the play marks her out as a keenly intelligent and witty woman. In lines 23–70 the Messenger does not know quite what has hit him!

a **'You must not, sir, mistake my niece'** Three of you take the parts of the Messenger, Leonato and Hero. The rest share out Beatrice's lines and sit around the Messenger, mocking him and deliberately 'mistaking' his meaning. You will find many other kinds of 'mistakings' presented in the play.

b **What does Beatrice think of 'Signor Mountanto' (i.e. Benedick)?** 'Mountanto' was a fencing term, which Beatrice uses here to imply Benedick is a flashy swordsman. Read through lines 23–70, changing speakers with each change of character. List all the 'failings' Beatrice says Benedick has. Does she like or dislike him?

---

set . . . bills posted notices
at the flight to an archery contest
subscribed signed on behalf of
birdbolt blunt-headed arrow
tax criticise
be meet get even
musty victual stale food

holp helped
trencherman good eater
wits parts of the mind
halting limping
next block latest hat shape
 (see p. 170)

4

BEATRICE I pray you, is Signor Mountanto returned from the wars or no?

MESSENGER I know none of that name, lady, there was none such in the
    army of any sort.   25

LEONATO What is he that you ask for, niece?

HERO My cousin means Signor Benedick of Padua.

MESSENGER O he's returned, and as pleasant as ever he was.

BEATRICE He set up his bills here in Messina, and challenged Cupid at
    the flight: and my uncle's fool, reading the challenge, subscribed for   30
    Cupid, and challenged him at the birdbolt. I pray you, how many hath
    he killed and eaten in these wars? But how many hath he killed? – for
    indeed I promised to eat all of his killing.

LEONATO Faith, niece, you tax Signor Benedick too much, but he'll be
    meet with you, I doubt it not.   35

MESSENGER He hath done good service, lady, in these wars.

BEATRICE You had musty victual, and he hath holp to eat it: he is a very
    valiant trencherman, he hath an excellent stomach.

MESSENGER And a good soldier too, lady.

BEATRICE And a good soldier to a lady, but what is he to a lord?   40

MESSENGER A lord to a lord, a man to a man, stuffed with all honourable
    virtues.

BEATRICE It is so indeed, he is no less than a stuffed man, but for the
    stuffing – well, we are all mortal.

LEONATO You must not, sir, mistake my niece: there is a kind of merry   45
    war betwixt Signor Benedick and her: they never meet but there's a
    skirmish of wit between them.

BEATRICE Alas, he gets nothing by that. In our last conflict, four of his
    five wits went halting off, and now is the whole man governed with
    one: so that if he have wit enough to keep himself warm, let him bear it   50
    for a difference between himself and his horse, for it is all the wealth
    that he hath left to be known a reasonable creature. Who is his
    companion now? He hath every month a new sworn brother.

MESSENGER Is't possible?

BEATRICE Very easily possible: he wears his faith but as the fashion of his   55
    hat, it ever changes with the next block.

As Beatrice continues to speak mockingly of Benedick to the Messenger, the prince, Don Pedro, and his followers arrive. Leonato eloquently welcomes his royal guest and Beatrice begins her taunting of Benedick.

1 Prepare to play the Messenger

This is a good role for a novice actor because his part is over by line 70! Study your lines and write notes on how you would play him (e.g. keen and eager, pompous and self-important, comic). What does he think of the governor and his niece Beatrice? Give reasons and evidence for your interpretation of his character.

2 The warriors return (in groups of nine or more)

Create your own version of lines 66–88 where Leonato welcomes the prince and his comrades in arms (see picture on page vi (bottom) in the colour section). Decide how best to spark off the exchange between Beatrice and Benedick. In one production Benedick bent down and accidentally prodded Beatrice with his sword.

Benedick is far left, in the plumed hat. Beatrice stands centre stage, half hidden behind the cypress tree. Why has the director placed her there?

---

your books   your good books
and he were   if he were
study   library
squarer   brawler, hooligan
pestilence   plague
taker   one who catches it
presently   immediately

ere a be   before he is
charge   trouble, expense
have it full   are well answered
fathers herself   i.e. looks like her father
marks   takes any notice of
Lady Disdain   contemptuous lady

MESSENGER I see, lady, the gentleman is not in your books.

BEATRICE No, and he were, I would burn my study. But I pray you, who is his companion? Is there no young squarer now, that will make a voyage with him to the devil? 60

MESSENGER He is most in the company of the right noble Claudio.

BEATRICE O Lord, he will hang upon him like a disease: he is sooner caught than the pestilence, and the taker runs presently mad. God help the noble Claudio, if he hath caught the Benedict. It will cost him a thousand pound ere a be cured. 65

MESSENGER I will hold friends with you, lady.

BEATRICE Do, good friend.

LEONATO You will never run mad, niece.

BEATRICE No, not till a hot January.

MESSENGER Don Pedro is approached. 70

Enter DON PEDRO, CLAUDIO, BENEDICK, BALTHASAR *and* JOHN *the bastard*

DON PEDRO Good Signor Leonato, are you come to meet your trouble? The fashion of the world is to avoid cost, and you encounter it.

LEONATO Never came trouble to my house in the likeness of your grace: for trouble being gone, comfort should remain: but when you depart from me, sorrow abides, and happiness takes his leave. 75

DON PEDRO You embrace your charge too willingly. I think this is your daughter?

LEONATO Her mother hath many times told me so.

BENEDICK Were you in doubt, sir, that you asked her?

LEONATO Signor Benedick, no, for then were you a child. 80

DON PEDRO You have it full, Benedick: we may guess by this, what you are, being a man. Truly, the lady fathers herself: be happy, lady, for you are like an honourable father.

BENEDICK If Signor Leonato be her father, she would not have his head on her shoulders for all Messina, as like him as she is. 85

BEATRICE I wonder that you will still be talking, Signor Benedick, nobody marks you.

BENEDICK What, my dear Lady Disdain! Are you yet living?

Beatrice and Benedick renew their 'merry war', each trying to score points off the other, each attempting to have the last word. Leonato invites Don Pedro and his followers to stay as guests at his house.

1 Show Beatrice and Benedick hurling insults (in pairs)

Beatrice once again interrupts the men's conversation. But this time she faces Benedick, a much more formidable opponent.

Face your partner and read lines 86–107 until you are comfortable with speaking the words.

Select the most insulting or amusing phrases your character uses each time they speak and compile a shortened script using just these phrases (with perhaps a few extra words of your own to help it all make sense). Then use your script to hurl the insults back and forth.

Show your version to the rest of the class. Decide who is forced to break off hostilities first and whether there is a clear winner to this particular skirmish in the 'merry war'.

2 Meet the villain (in groups of three)

A character's first words are often very revealing. It was Don John who led the recent rebellion against his brother, Don Pedro, although the two are now friends again ('reconciled'). Write notes for the actors advising them on how to make lines 113–18 an uneasy moment in an otherwise happy reunion. How do you think the two royal brothers should behave towards each other?

Courtesy . . . presence even courtesy itself would be rude to you
turn-coat traitor
dear happiness great good fortune
pernicious evil, villainous
humour temperament
scape . . . face escape the fate of getting his face scratched
and 'twere if it were
parrot-teacher chatterer
so . . . continuer were as good at keeping going
jade broken-down vicious horse
be forsworn swear in vain

BEATRICE Is it possible Disdain should die, while she hath such meet
food to feed it, as Signor Benedick? Courtesy itself must convert to   90
Disdain, if you come in her presence.

BENEDICK Then is Courtesy a turn-coat: but it is certain I am loved of all
ladies, only you excepted: and I would I could find in my heart that I
had not a hard heart, for truly I love none.

BEATRICE A dear happiness to women, they would else have been   95
troubled with a pernicious suitor. I thank God and my cold blood, I
am of your humour for that: I had rather hear my dog bark at a crow
than a man swear he loves me.

BENEDICK God keep your ladyship still in that mind, so some gentleman
or other shall scape a predestinate scratched face.   100

BEATRICE Scratching could not make it worse, and 'twere such a face as
yours were.

BENEDICK Well, you are a rare parrot-teacher.

BEATRICE A bird of my tongue is better than a beast of yours.

BENEDICK I would my horse had the speed of your tongue, and so good a   105
continuer: but keep your way a God's name. I have done.

BEATRICE You always end with a jade's trick: I know you of old.

DON PEDRO That is the sum of all: Leonato, Signor Claudio and Signor
Benedick, my dear friend Leonato, hath invited you all. I tell him we
still stay here at the least a month, and he heartily prays some   110
occasion may detain us longer. I dare swear he is no hypocrite, but
prays from his heart.

LEONATO If you swear, my lord, you shall not be forsworn. [*To Don John*]
Let me bid you welcome, my lord, being reconciled to the prince your
brother: I owe you all duty.   115

DON JOHN I thank you, I am not of many words, but I thank you.

LEONATO Please it your grace lead on?

DON PEDRO Your hand, Leonato, we will go together.

Exeunt all except Benedick and Claudio

Claudio tells Benedick of his love for Hero and asks Benedick what he thinks of her. Benedick is unimpressed by Hero's charms and quite dismayed that his young friend Claudio should be considering marriage.

1 Innocent youth and worldly experience (in pairs)

Take parts and read aloud lines 119–50. Choose three sections where Claudio talks very seriously about his new love and Benedick teasingly refuses to take his friend seriously. Rehearse your sections and show them to the class.

Count Claudio is very much Benedick's social superior. Does he behave as though he is? Benedick is often played as being slightly older than Claudio. Does he sound older to you?

2 Benedick the witty woman-hater (in small groups)

In lines 136–7, Benedick pretends to think that Claudio is mocking him by making impossible remarks (Cupid, the god of love, was blind; Vulcan, the god of fire, was a blacksmith).

a Find other examples of Benedick's agility of mind and love of play-acting on this page. Has he made any genuinely serious remarks since he appeared?

b 'Shall I never see a bachelor of three score again?', says Benedick the apparently cynical woman-hater (lines 147–8). Find clues that suggest he is more susceptible to women than he would care to admit.

3 Noting or nothing?

The play's title has a double meaning. 'Nothing' and 'noting' sounded very similar in Shakespeare's time. Both Claudio and Benedick talk of 'noting' (observing) Leonato's daughter. You will find that the play will be full of 'notings' as well as 'nothings'.

---

noted her not   did not study her
modest   sweet, virginal, innocent
low   short
flouting Jack   mocking rascal
go in the song   match your mood
and she . . . fury   if only she were not so tormenting

wear his cap   i.e. to hide his cuckold's horns (see p. 12)
and thou wilt needs   if you must
yoke   a wooden frame to harness pairs of oxen
sigh away Sundays   be stuck at home with the wife on Sundays

CLAUDIO Benedick, didst thou note the daughter of Signor Leonato?

BENEDICK I noted her not, but I looked on her. *quiet* 120

CLAUDIO Is she not a modest young lady?

BENEDICK Do you question me as an honest man should do, for my simple true judgement? Or would you have me speak after my custom, as being a professed tyrant to their sex?

CLAUDIO No, I pray thee speak in sober judgement. 125

BENEDICK Why i'faith, methinks she's too low for a high praise, too brown for a fair praise, and too little for a great praise. Only this commendation I can afford her, that were she other than she is, she were unhandsome, and being no other, but as she is – I do not like her. 130

CLAUDIO Thou thinkest I am in sport. I pray thee, tell me truly how thou lik'st her?

BENEDICK Would you buy her, that you enquire after her?

CLAUDIO Can the world buy such a jewel?

BENEDICK Yea, and a case to put it into. But speak you this with a sad 135
brow? Or do you play the flouting Jack, to tell us Cupid is a good hare-finder, and Vulcan a rare carpenter? Come, in what key shall a man take you, to go in the song?

CLAUDIO In mine eye, she is the sweetest lady that ever I looked on.

Judging by her looks

BENEDICK I can see yet without spectacles, and I see no such matter. 140
There's her cousin, and she were not possessed with a fury, exceeds her as much in beauty as the first of May doth the last of December. But I hope you have no intent to turn husband, have you?

CLAUDIO I would scarce trust myself, though I had sworn the contrary, if Hero would be my wife. 145

BENEDICK Is't come to this? In faith, hath not the world one man, but he will wear his cap with suspicion? Shall I never see a bachelor of three score again? Go to, i'faith, and thou wilt needs thrust thy neck into a yoke, wear the print of it, and sigh away Sundays. Look, Don Pedro is returned to seek you. 150

Claudio's love is conventional.

Don Pedro returns to find out why his friends have stayed behind. Benedick reveals that Claudio is secretly in love with Hero and vows that he himself will never be so foolish as to be tempted into marriage.

1 Comrades in arms (in groups of three)

Here are three men who have been through the war together. They are alone and relaxed. Read lines 151–215, each playing one of the three friends. Speak and react in the way you imagine these military men would. Benedick should be as 'non-serious' as ever. How like today's young men are they, particularly in their talk of love?

2 Too serious to joke about?

Like many Elizabethan aristocrats, these friends are enjoying showing off their education and skill with words, making jokes, even about matters deeply important to Elizabethans such as love, religion, allegiance and troth (honour). Find examples from lines 151–215 of the three men playing lightheartedly with these concerns.

Horns and cuckolds   A favourite object of ridicule for the Elizabethans was the cuckold, a man whose wife was unfaithful to him. The cuckold was supposed to grow horns on his forehead, invisible to himself but obvious to everyone else, hence Benedick's remark about the married man needing to wear a cap (line 147).

a   Work out how Benedick elaborates on this idea in lines 178–82. Remember, bugles or hunting horns were originally made from actual animal horns; a 'recheat' is a hunting call; 'winded' means blown or played; and a 'baldrick' is a belt.

b   The cuckold may have been a male figure of fun, but what does this conversation suggest to you about Elizabethan attitudes to women?

---

allegiance   duty to your lord
your . . . part   the question your lordship is supposed to ask
fetch me in   trick me
troth   honour, truth, faith
worthy   estimable, of high status

die . . . stake   be burnt at the stake for my religious beliefs
the despite of   your contempt for
maintain . . . will   keep up his pretence (of being a woman-hater) except by will-power
fine   conclusion

Enter DON PEDRO

DON PEDRO What secret hath held you here, that you followed not to
Leonato's?

BENEDICK I would your grace would constrain me to tell.

DON PEDRO I charge thee on thy allegiance.

BENEDICK You hear, Count Claudio, I can be secret as a dumb man – I   155
would have you think so. But on my allegiance (mark you this, on my
allegiance) he is in love. With who? Now that is your grace's part:
mark how short his answer is. With Hero, Leonato's short daughter.

CLAUDIO If this were so, so were it uttered.

BENEDICK Like the old tale, my lord: 'It is not so, nor 'twas not so, but   160
indeed, God forbid it should be so.'

CLAUDIO If my passion change not shortly, God forbid it should be
otherwise.

DON PEDRO Amen, if you love her, for the lady is very well worthy.

CLAUDIO You speak this to fetch me in, my lord.   165

DON PEDRO By my troth, I speak my thought.

CLAUDIO And in faith, my lord, I spoke mine.

BENEDICK And by my two faiths and troths, my lord, I spoke mine.

CLAUDIO That I love her, I feel.

DON PEDRO That she is worthy, I know.   170

BENEDICK That I neither feel how she should be loved, nor know how
she should be worthy, is the opinion that fire cannot melt out of me: I
will die in it at the stake.

DON PEDRO Thou wast ever an obstinate heretic in the despite of beauty.

CLAUDIO And never could maintain his part, but in the force of his   175
will.

BENEDICK That a woman conceived me, I thank her: that she brought
me up, I likewise give her most humble thanks: but that I will have a
recheat winded in my forehead, or hang my bugle in an invisible
baldrick, all women shall pardon me. Because I will not do them the   180
wrong to mistrust any, I will do myself the right to trust none: and the
fine is (for the which I may go the finer) I will live a bachelor.

Don Pedro predicts that Benedick will also one day fall in love. Supremely confident, Benedick lays down a challenge: his friends can do all manner of things to ridicule him if he ever does fall for a woman's charms.

---

1 'Benedick the married man' (in small groups)

Draw pictures of the three things that Benedick promises they may do to him if he falls in love (lines 184–99). Share your ideas with the group. Many people joke about things that disturb or worry them. Is Benedick genuinely antagonistic to women, or masking his fear of commitment?

2 Jokes about writing letters (in groups of three)

Much Elizabethan humour depends on knowledge that a modern audience no longer possesses. Benedick says 'so I commit you–' (line 209), which was also an Elizabethan way of ending a letter. Claudio and Don Pedro pick up Benedick's words and mockingly answer in similar letter-style.

Where possible, actors bring this humour to life with gestures, expressions and stage 'business'. Take a part each and memorise lines 205–12 (from 'good Signor Benedick' to 'Nay, mock not, mock not'). Devise a presentation to the class which makes the letter joke clear to your audience. Can you make them laugh?

3 Fashions and outward show

Benedick is not going to leave without having the last word. He says that his friends' mocking use of conventional letter endings ('ere you flout old ends any further') resembles the trimmings ('guards') which have been only loosely sewn ('basted') onto the body of a garment.

Benedick is joking here, but costume and dress will assume a serious and almost tragic importance in future events. Many characters will adopt masks and disguises; many will attempt to judge a person's inner worth by their outward show.

---

lose . . . love sighing consumed blood, drinking replenished it
ballad-maker writer of love songs
sign . . . Cupid brothel sign
fall . . . faith change your beliefs
argument subject for discussion
bottle wicker basket

Adam a famous archer of the day
as time shall try time will tell
horn-mad raving mad
Venice noted for loose morals
temporise . . . hours change with time
tuition protection

DON PEDRO I shall see thee, ere I die, look pale with love.

BENEDICK With anger, with sickness, or with hunger, my lord, not with love: prove that ever I lose more blood with love than I will get again with drinking, pick out mine eyes with a ballad-maker's pen, and hang me up at the door of a brothel house for the sign of blind Cupid. 185

DON PEDRO Well, if ever thou dost fall from this faith, thou wilt prove a notable argument. 190

BENEDICK If I do, hang me in a bottle like a cat, and shoot at me, and he that hits me, let him be clapped on the shoulder, and called Adam.

DON PEDRO Well, as time shall try: 'In time the savage bull doth bear the yoke.'

BENEDICK The savage bull may, but if ever the sensible Benedick bear it, 195 pluck off the bull's horns, and set them in my forehead, and let me be vilely painted, and in such great letters as they write, 'Here is good horse to hire', let them signify under my sign, 'Here you may see Benedick the married man.'

CLAUDIO If this should ever happen, thou wouldst be horn-mad. 200

DON PEDRO Nay, if Cupid have not spent all his quiver in Venice, thou wilt quake for this shortly.

BENEDICK I look for an earthquake too then.

DON PEDRO Well, you will temporise with the hours. In the mean time, good Signor Benedick, repair to Leonato's, commend me to him, and 205 tell him I will not fail him at supper, for indeed he hath made great preparation.

BENEDICK I have almost matter enough in me for such an embassage, and so I commit you –

CLAUDIO To the tuition of God: from my house if I had it – 210

DON PEDRO The sixth of July: your loving friend Benedick.

BENEDICK Nay, mock not, mock not: the body of your discourse is sometime guarded with fragments, and the guards are but slightly basted on, neither: ere you flout old ends any further, examine your conscience: and so I leave you.   *Exit* 215

Claudio confesses how much his love for Hero has grown since their return from the war. The prince offers to help him win her. That night at the masked ball he will pretend to be Claudio and woo Hero on his behalf.

---

1 The soldier becomes the lover (in large groups)

In lines 223–31 Claudio tells Don Pedro that he saw and liked Hero before they set off on their campaign, but thoughts of war were too pressing to allow thoughts of love to grow. Now the war is over, Hero's charms cannot be denied.

a Find out how words about love and war echo through their language. Two of you take the parts of Claudio and Don Pedro and read slowly lines 224–54. The rest divide into two groups. One group listens for and repeats all the 'soft/love' words. The other group listens for and echoes all the 'rough/war' words. The two groups of words coincide near the end of this scene. What does this tell you about male notions of how to woo a woman?

b Does Claudio genuinely love Hero? Find the line on the opposite page which suggests he is not only interested in Hero's beauty and charm.

2 Witty prose changes to romantic blank verse (in pairs)

Up to the departure of Benedick, characters have talked in elegant and witty prose. Now Claudio and Don Pedro begin to speak in blank (unrhymed) verse.

Take a part each, sit face to face and read aloud lines 216–54. Practise speaking your lines with rhythm and expression (p. 188 will help you with the structure of blank verse). Then select your favourite lines and rehearse speaking them with passion and sincerity. Present your selections to the class.

---

apt eager, quick
affect care for
break broach the subject
his complexion its appearance
salved it expressed it more gently
treatise account, explanation

What need . . . flood? a bridge need only be as broad as the river
The fairest . . . necessity the best gift is one that meets the need
Look what whatever
'tis once in a word
fit thee provide you

CLAUDIO My liege, your highness now may do me good.

DON PEDRO My love is thine to teach, teach it but how,
⠀⠀⠀⠀⠀⠀⠀And thou shalt see how apt it is to learn
⠀⠀⠀⠀⠀⠀⠀Any hard lesson that may do thee good.

CLAUDIO Hath Leonato any son, my lord?⠀⠀⠀⠀⠀⠀⠀⠀⠀⠀⠀⠀220

DON PEDRO No child but Hero, she's his only heir:
⠀⠀⠀⠀⠀⠀⠀Dost thou affect her, Claudio?

CLAUDIO⠀⠀⠀⠀⠀⠀⠀⠀⠀⠀⠀⠀⠀⠀⠀O my lord,
⠀⠀⠀⠀⠀⠀⠀When you went onward on this ended action,
⠀⠀⠀⠀⠀⠀⠀I looked upon her with a soldier's eye,
⠀⠀⠀⠀⠀⠀⠀That liked, but had a rougher task in hand,⠀⠀⠀⠀225
⠀⠀⠀⠀⠀⠀⠀Than to drive liking to the name of love;
⠀⠀⠀⠀⠀⠀⠀But now I am returned, and that war-thoughts
⠀⠀⠀⠀⠀⠀⠀Have left their places vacant, in their rooms
⠀⠀⠀⠀⠀⠀⠀Come thronging soft and delicate desires,
⠀⠀⠀⠀⠀⠀⠀All prompting me how fair young Hero is,⠀⠀⠀⠀230
⠀⠀⠀⠀⠀⠀⠀Saying I liked her ere I went to wars.

DON PEDRO Thou wilt be like a lover presently,
⠀⠀⠀⠀⠀⠀⠀And tire the hearer with a book of words:
⠀⠀⠀⠀⠀⠀⠀If thou dost love fair Hero, cherish it,
⠀⠀⠀⠀⠀⠀⠀And I will break with her, and with her father,⠀⠀235
⠀⠀⠀⠀⠀⠀⠀And thou shalt have her. Wast not to this end,
⠀⠀⠀⠀⠀⠀⠀That thou began'st to twist so fine a story?

CLAUDIO How sweetly you do minister to love,
⠀⠀⠀⠀⠀⠀⠀That know love's grief by his complexion!
⠀⠀⠀⠀⠀⠀⠀But lest my liking might too sudden seem,⠀⠀⠀⠀240
⠀⠀⠀⠀⠀⠀⠀I would have salved it with a longer treatise.

DON PEDRO What need the bridge much broader than the flood?
⠀⠀⠀⠀⠀⠀⠀The fairest grant is the necessity.
⠀⠀⠀⠀⠀⠀⠀Look what will serve is fit: 'tis once, thou lovest,
⠀⠀⠀⠀⠀⠀⠀And I will fit thee with the remedy.⠀⠀⠀⠀⠀⠀⠀⠀245
⠀⠀⠀⠀⠀⠀⠀I know we shall have revelling tonight,
⠀⠀⠀⠀⠀⠀⠀I will assume thy part in some disguise,
⠀⠀⠀⠀⠀⠀⠀And tell fair Hero I am Claudio,
⠀⠀⠀⠀⠀⠀⠀And in her bosom I'll unclasp my heart,
⠀⠀⠀⠀⠀⠀⠀And take her hearing prisoner with the force⠀⠀⠀250
⠀⠀⠀⠀⠀⠀⠀And strong encounter of my amorous tale:
⠀⠀⠀⠀⠀⠀⠀Then after, to her father will I break,
⠀⠀⠀⠀⠀⠀⠀And the conclusion is, she shall be thine:
⠀⠀⠀⠀⠀⠀⠀In practice let us put it presently.

⠀⠀⠀⠀⠀⠀⠀⠀⠀⠀⠀⠀⠀⠀⠀⠀⠀⠀⠀⠀⠀⠀⠀⠀⠀*Exeunt*

Antonio tells Leonato that Don Pedro's conversation with Claudio has been overheard. Apparently, the prince is in love with Hero and plans that very evening at the masked ball to ask for her hand in marriage.

---

1 How easily are we deceived by appearances? (in pairs)

Leonato's brother, Antonio, seems convinced by his servant's report that it is Don Pedro who loves Hero and wants to marry her! This is just the first of many eavesdroppings, mistaken conclusions and misreportings in the play.

a Read the scene through several times, taking a part each. Speak to your brother as though you were both discussing an exciting rumour that you don't want others to know you know. Is Leonato as easily convinced by the servant's story as Antonio seems to be?

b Find two phrases which specifically refer to outward appearances. How many similar phrases can you find in the opening lines of the play (Act 1 Scene 1, lines 1–22)?

2 Prepare for the supper (in small groups)

As the stage direction ('*Several persons cross the stage*') indicates, this scene ends with great hustle and bustle as Leonato and his household get ready for the banquet and dancing

Imagine you are directing the play. Write notes for lines 13–21 on how the actors, especially the non-speaking ones, are to create an atmosphere of domestic activity.

3 'I will acquaint my daughter withal'

Compare the merits of Don Pedro and Claudio as prospective husbands. Has Hero said or done anything so far to give you a clue as to her preferred choice? Which man might her father Leonato favour?

How now   Hello, what news?
cousin   kinsman
As the events stamps them   it depends on the outcome
cover   outward appearance
thick-pleached   hedged, wooded
discovered   revealed

accordant   in agreement
take . . . top   seize the opportunity
break . . . it   discuss it with you
appear itself   actually happens
peradventure   perhaps
cry you mercy   beg your pardon

Act 1 Scene 2
Leonato's house

Enter LEONATO and an old man ANTONIO, brother to Leonato

LEONATO How now, brother, where is my cousin your son? Hath he
provided this music?

ANTONIO He is very busy about it: but, brother, I can tell you strange
news that you yet dreamed not of.

LEONATO Are they good?   5

ANTONIO As the events stamps them, but they have a good cover: they
show well outward. The prince and Count Claudio walking in a
thick-pleached alley in mine orchard, were thus much overheard by a
man of mine: the prince discovered to Claudio that he loved my niece
your daughter, and meant to acknowledge it this night in a dance, and   10
if he found her accordant, he meant to take the present time by the
top, and instantly break with you of it.

LEONATO Hath the fellow any wit that told you this?

ANTONIO A good sharp fellow, I will send for him, and question him
yourself.   15

LEONATO No, no, we will hold it as a dream till it appear itself: but I will
acquaint my daughter withal, that she may be the better prepared for
an answer, if peradventure this be true; go you, and tell her of it.
[Several persons cross the stage]
Cousins, you know what you have to do. O I cry you mercy, friend, go
you with me and I will use your skill: good cousin, have a care this   20
busy time.

Exeunt

Full of malice and ill-humour, Don John has chosen not to attend the supper. Conrade urges him to avoid causing further offence now that he has so few friends left, but Don John's bitter anger will not be softened.

1 The 'plain-dealing villain' (in groups of three)

The opening stage direction describes Don John as 'the bastard'. In Shakespeare's day, a person born outside marriage was expected to be jealous, scheming and bad-tempered (see p. 179). Take a part each and read the whole scene.

a What part has 'the bastard' played in the recent war and why is he so resentful of his brother and of Claudio?

b Don John says (lines 8–10) that Conrade, born under the planet Saturn, should be sour and gloomy like himself. Do you think Conrade is like this?

c Speak Don John's 'thought-lists'. Read aloud lines 8–13 and 20–7, handing over to the next person at the end of each thought (generally marked by a full stop or colon). Emphasise the patterns in Don John's words. What sort of villain does he sound like?

2 Happiness turns to menace (in groups of four)

On Shakespeare's stage the action probably flowed quickly from scene to scene. Indeed, the earliest published versions of his plays did not divide the script into separate acts or scenes at all.

Two of you play Leonato and Antonio, the other two play Don John and Conrade. Rehearse your version of the final few lines of Scene 2 together with the first few lines of Scene 3. Make the action flow without a break, but emphasise the change of atmosphere. Present your version to the rest of the class.

What . . . year   What the devil!
out of measure   excessively
present   immediate, quick
moral medicine   words of advice
mortifying mischief   fatal disease
claw   flatter
without controlment   freely

stood out   rebelled
frame   bring about
canker   wild rose
fashion a carriage   put on an act
enfranchised   set free
clog   heavy wooden block (used to tether animals)

Act 1 Scene 3
Outside Leonato's house

Enter DON JOHN the bastard and CONRADE his companion

CONRADE What the good year, my lord, why are you thus out of measure
sad?

DON JOHN There is no measure in the occasion that breeds, therefore the
sadness is without limit.

CONRADE You should hear reason.   5

DON JOHN And when I have heard it, what blessing brings it?

CONRADE If not a present remedy, at least a patient sufferance.

DON JOHN I wonder that thou (being as thou sayest thou art, born under
Saturn) goest about to apply a moral medicine to a mortifying
mischief. I cannot hide what I am: I must be sad when I have cause,   10
and smile at no man's jests: eat when I have stomach, and wait for no
man's leisure: sleep when I am drowsy, and tend on no man's
business: laugh when I am merry, and claw no man in his humour.

CONRADE Yea, but you must not make the full show of this till you may do
it without controlment. You have of late stood out against your   15
brother, and he hath ta'en you newly into his grace, where it is
impossible you should take true root, but by the fair weather that you
make yourself: it is needful that you frame the season for your own
harvest.

DON JOHN I had rather be a canker in a hedge, than a rose in his grace,   20
and it better fits my blood to be disdained of all, than to fashion a
carriage to rob love from any. In this (though I cannot be said to be a
flattering honest man) it must not be denied but I am a plain-dealing
villain. I am trusted with a muzzle, and enfranchised with a clog,
therefore I have decreed not to sing in my cage. If I had my mouth, I   25
would bite: if I had my liberty, I would do my liking. In the mean time,
let me be that I am, and seek not to alter me.

CONRADE Can you make no use of your discontent?

DON JOHN I make all use of it, for I use it only. Who comes here?

Borachio comes from the great supper and tells of Don Pedro's plan to woo Hero on Claudio's behalf. Don John decides to use this information to get his revenge on Claudio, whom he particularly hates.

1 Do the men in the play hate or love women?

Don Pedro's disaffected brother is clearly a woman-hater. 'What is he for a fool that betroths himself to unquietness?', says Don John (lines 34–5), meaning 'What kind of fool wishes to get married and give himself nothing but worry?' Which other man has expressed similarly misogynistic (women-hating) attitudes? Be alert to other examples of hostile male attitudes to women as the play progresses.

This is how one production portrayed Don John. Another production dressed him to look like Napoleon. Which actor from film, television or theatre would you choose to play him? What would be your choice of costume and make-up?

2 Show Don John's dearest wish (in large groups)

'Would the cook were a my mind', says Don John as he leaves for the banquet (line 53). Devise a mime version of what Don John dearly wishes to happen at the banquet.

for any model as a design	**smoking** fumigating
forward March-chick precocious youngster	**arras** wall-hangings
	start-up upstart
Being . . . perfumer instructed to make the rooms sweet-smelling	**were a my mind** thought like me
	go prove go and find out

Enter BORACHIO

What news, Borachio?   30

BORACHIO I came yonder from a great supper, the prince your brother is
royally entertained by Leonato, and I can give you intelligence of an
intended marriage.

DON JOHN Will it serve for any model to build mischief on? What is he for
a fool that betroths himself to unquietness?   35

BORACHIO Marry, it is your brother's right hand.

DON JOHN Who, the most exquisite Claudio?

BORACHIO Even he.

DON JOHN A proper squire! And who, and who, which way looks he?

BORACHIO Marry, on Hero, the daughter and heir of Leonato.   40

DON JOHN A very forward March-chick. How came you to this?

BORACHIO Being entertained for a perfumer, as I was smoking a musty
room, comes me the prince and Claudio, hand in hand, in sad
conference: I whipped me behind the arras, and there heard it agreed
upon, that the prince should woo Hero for himself, and having   45
obtained her, give her to Count Claudio.

DON JOHN Come, come, let us thither, this may prove food to my
displeasure, that young start-up hath all the glory of my overthrow: if I
can cross him any way, I bless myself every way. You are both sure,
and will assist me?   50

CONRADE To the death, my lord.

DON JOHN Let us to the great supper, their cheer is the greater that I am
subdued. Would the cook were a my mind: shall we go prove what's to
be done?

BORACHIO We'll wait upon your lordship.   55

Exeunt

Looking back at Act 1
Activities for groups or individuals

---

1 Tell the story of Act 1 (in groups of five to eight)

The gossip columnist One of you is a gossip columnist. Your sources
of information are queuing up to tell you of the latest news and
scandal amongst Messina society. The other group members make a
list of different pieces of news from Act 1. Each in turn tells the
gossip columnist a piece of news. The gossip columnist should
cross-examine each of the informants to make sure the details are
correct.

The Messenger The Messenger returns to his regiment and tells his
friends about the news he carried to Leonato. He then gives them his
impressions of Leonato, Hero and Beatrice. As he relates his story,
his friends question him about the characters, the events and the
household he describes.

2 Three comrades in arms (in groups of three)

Benedick, Don Pedro and Claudio seem to be good friends. They have,
after all, just fought together against Don John.

Choose a character each. Make a large outline drawing of your
character and inside it write:

- your status in relation to your two friends
- what you have in common with your friends
- the ways in which you are different from your friends
- what binds you together.

Show your drawings to each other and swap your ideas about these
three men.

3 The villain masked and unmasked

When his brother is present, Don John has to mask his ill-feeling.
However, Shakespeare often gives his villains opportunities to confess
their secret thoughts to the audience. Write a monologue for Don
John, which he might speak at the end of Act 1 Scene 3 after Borachio
and Conrade have left. Write it in the same style of prose that Don
John uses earlier in the scene.

4 What does Benedick think of Beatrice?

Here we see Benedick the returning soldier, apparently carefree and immune to love. But is he?

What does he really think of Beatrice and what are his thoughts after their latest 'skirmish of wit'? Write two extracts from Benedick's diary: one written that evening and one written after an earlier meeting with Beatrice before he went away to war.

5 A comic web of friends, cousins, lovers and haters

Characters in Shakespearian comedy often behave like figures in a dance, forming patterns of relationships which dissolve and re-form as the play progresses. Act 1 is concerned with young people (Claudio, Benedick, Hero and Beatrice) and the seriously enjoyable matters of friendship, falling in love and getting married.

Make notes on the patterns of relationships forming between these four characters. For example, how does the 'love' pair, Claudio and Hero, compare with the 'love–hate' pair, Beatrice and Benedick? How does Beatrice contrast with her cousin Hero and how much alike are Benedick and his friend Claudio? You may wish to present your findings as a diagram or chart.

6 Why is Beatrice so aggressive and Hero so silent?

There are many powerful men in this play: two princes and a count, a signor and a governor. Look back at Act 1 Scene 1 and decide how each young woman copes in such potentially intimidating male company.

Beatrice and Hero are very good friends in this play. Write a paragraph explaining why two such contrasting personalities might become so close.

Beatrice describes her ideal man, remarking how poorly Don John and Benedick match up to her requirements. Leonato warns her that such talk will not get her a husband, but Beatrice says she is happy to stay single.

1 A private family moment (in groups of four)

This scene opens with a glimpse into the governor's family life. How complex are this family's relationships? Take a part each (including the silent Hero).

a **Conversation or battle?** Read lines 1–60 in two ways: first as a relaxed and leisurely family conversation, and then more forcefully as though you were engaged in a battle of wits and opinions. Which way seems to work better? The silent Hero must give her opinion of what she hears.

b **Play the family relationship game** Read lines 1–60 together. Think carefully about who says what to whom, then prepare to make statements, in role, to the other three. To each character in turn you must state your name, describe yourself and your relationship to them, give your opinion of them, and finally compare your view of marriage with what you believe is theirs. When you finish speaking to a character, he or she must immediately reply to you in the same way. The pattern could be something as simple as:

> My name is . . . I am an old/young . . . I am your . . . I think you are . . . Marriage is . . . .

2 Beatrice will lead the bear-keeper's apes into hell

According to the Elizabethans, this was the traditional fate of all old maids (line 31). No one knows how this idea came into being. Write a paragraph giving your own explanation for this strange belief.

---

tartly   sourly
image   statue
foot/purse/will/horns   (see p. 28)
if a could   if he could
shrewd   shrewish, or sharp
curst   ill-natured, foul
 tempered

lessen God's sending   reduce what
 God has given me
Just   just so
at him   praying to God
the woollen   scratchy blankets
in earnest of the bearward   as a
 token payment from the bear-keeper

Act 2 Scene 1
The great chamber of Leonato's house

Enter LEONATO, *his brother* ANTONIO, HERO *his daughter and*
BEATRICE his niece

LEONATO Was not Count John here at supper?

ANTONIO I saw him not.

BEATRICE How tartly that gentleman looks, I never can see him but I am
heart-burned an hour after.

HERO He is of a very melancholy disposition.   5

BEATRICE He were an excellent man that were made just in the mid-way
between him and Benedick: the one is too like an image and says
nothing, and the other too like my lady's eldest son, evermore tattling.

LEONATO Then half Signor Benedick's tongue in Count John's mouth,
and half Count John's melancholy in Signor Benedick's face –   10

BEATRICE With a good leg and a good foot, uncle, and money enough in
his purse, such a man would win any woman in the world if a could get
her good will.

LEONATO By my troth, niece, thou wilt never get thee a husband, if thou
be so shrewd of thy tongue.   15

ANTONIO In faith, she's too curst.

BEATRICE Too curst is more than curst, I shall lessen God's sending that
way: for it is said, God sends a curst cow short horns, but to a cow too
curst, he sends none.

LEONATO So, by being too curst, God will send you no horns.   20

BEATRICE Just, if he send me no husband, for the which blessing I am at
him upon my knees every morning and evening: Lord, I could not
endure a husband with a beard on his face, I had rather lie in the
woollen!

LEONATO You may light on a husband that hath no beard.   25

BEATRICE What should I do with him – dress him in my apparel and
make him my waiting gentlewoman? He that hath a beard is more
than a youth: and he that hath no beard is less than a man: and he that
is more than a youth, is not for me, and he that is less than a man, I am
not for him: therefore I will even take sixpence in earnest of the   30
bearward, and lead his apes into hell.

Beatrice mockingly advises Hero on when and when not to obey her father in the matter of marriage. She then gives her own views of courtship, weddings and the regrets of life after a hasty marriage.

1 What is the silent Hero thinking? (in groups of four)

Hero has been told that the prince will propose marriage to her this very evening. Will she accept? Why might she not dare to refuse?

Prepare a presentation of lines 38–57 in which Hero breaks her silence. After each sentence Hero adds her own comment (perhaps agreeing or disagreeing and explaining why).

2 'Wooing, wedding, and repenting' (in pairs)

Beatrice describes courtship and marriage as being like dances. Devise a mime based on lines 52–7 in which you woo, marry and repent in a series of dances:

- a Scotch jig: a lively dance ('hot and hasty')
- a measure: a slow, formal dance ('full of state and ancientry')
- a cinquepace (pronounced 'sink-a-pace'): a capering dance of five steps followed by a leap.

Show your version to the rest of the class or, if there is room, the whole class can dance out their versions together.

3 Beatrice's 'foul language'

Elizabethans would have enjoyed the game of sexual innuendo that Beatrice and Leonato play in lines 11–47. 'Will' could mean lust or the sexual organs, and 'foot' was a biblical euphemism for the penis. 'Purse', 'horns' and 'fitted' also possessed sexual overtones. What is your opinion of young women using such bawdy language? Does it change your view of Beatrice in any way?

Saint Peter guardian of the gates of heaven
metal substance
earth/dust/marl Beatrice plays with the idea that God created Adam, the first man, out of earth

match . . . kindred marry a close relative
solicit . . . kind i.e. propose marriage
important pushy, hasty
measure (1) moderation (2) dance
the first suit wooing
passing shrewdly very sharply

LEONATO Well then, go you into hell.

BEATRICE No, but to the gate, and there will the devil meet me like an old
    cuckold with horns on his head, and say, get you to heaven, Beatrice,
    get you to heaven, here's no place for you maids. So deliver I up my   35
    apes, and away to Saint Peter: for the heavens, he shows me where the
    bachelors sit, and there live we, as merry as the day is long.

ANTONIO Well, niece, I trust you will be ruled by your father.

BEATRICE Yes faith, it is my cousin's duty to make curtsy, and say, father,
    as it please you: but yet for all that, cousin, let him be a handsome   40
    fellow, or else make another curtsy, and say, father, as it please me.

LEONATO Well, niece, I hope to see you one day fitted with a husband.

BEATRICE Not till God make men of some other metal than earth: would
    it not grieve a woman to be overmastered with a piece of valiant dust?
    to make an account of her life to a clod of wayward marl? No, uncle,   45
    I'll none: Adam's sons are my brethren, and truly I hold it a sin to
    match in my kindred.

LEONATO Daughter, remember what I told you: if the prince do solicit
    you in that kind, you know your answer.

BEATRICE The fault will be in the music, cousin, if you be not wooed in   50
    good time: if the prince be too important, tell him there is measure in
    everything, and so dance out the answer. For hear me, Hero, wooing,
    wedding, and repenting, is as a Scotch jig, a measure and a
    cinquepace: the first suit is hot and hasty like a Scotch jig (and full as
    fantastical), the wedding mannerly modest (as a measure) full of state   55
    and ancientry, and then comes Repentance, and with his bad legs falls
    into the cinquepace faster and faster, till he sink into his grave.

LEONATO Cousin, you apprehend passing shrewdly.

BEATRICE I have a good eye, uncle, I can see a church by daylight.

LEONATO The revellers are entering, brother, make good room.   60

                                                [Exit Antonio]

Don Pedro, his friends and attendants enter wearing masks. The room fills with people and the masked dancing begins. As they dance, each woman uses the opportunity to mock her masked partner.

1 Take your partners! (in groups of six)

Masking was a favourite entertainment in great Elizabethan households. A group of masked male dancers would enter the chamber and take partners from the assembled guests (see the pictures on page viii in the colour section and on p. 32). Shakespeare has filled his masked dance with ill-matched couples. In pairs, choose one of the following activities:

a **The handsome prince?** Memorise lines 61–70. Hero believes that the masked Don Pedro will declare his love for her. Decide whether she wants him to or not and show her response.

b **Give him the brush-off** Memorise lines 71–81. Perhaps Margaret is very fond of another man? Show her resisting the masked Balthasar's advances.

c **Youth and age** Memorise lines 82–91. Show Ursula making fun of the masked Antonio. What are the old man's reactions?

Rehearse the three parts in sequence (perhaps with suitable music), as if you were in the middle of a dance, then show it to the rest of the class.

2 Hero speaks at last

Hero has barely spoken to anyone, yet here (lines 61–70) she more than holds her own with Don Pedro, even daring, perhaps, to mock his bald head! When he claims his mask, like Philemon's humble house, hides the god Jove (the Roman god Jupiter), Hero retorts, 'Why then your visor should be thatched' (see p. 183 for the story).

Why is Hero so talkative with the prince, when she has until now been virtually silent in male company?

---

walk a bout dance
So you so long as you
favour face
God defend . . . case I hope your face looks better than your mask
visor mask

Philemon's roof . . . thatched (see Activity 2 above and p. 183)
clerk church official who leads the responses to the prayers
counterfeit impersonate
up and down all over
Go to, mum come, say no more

Enter DON PEDRO, CLAUDIO, BENEDICK *and* BALTHASAR, *Maskers
with a drum;* [*re-enter* ANTONIO, *masked, followed by*] DON JOHN
[*and* BORACHIO *and others including* MARGARET
and URSULA. *The dance begins*]

DON PEDRO Lady, will you walk a bout with your friend?

HERO So you walk softly, and look sweetly, and say nothing, I am yours for
the walk, and especially when I walk away.

DON PEDRO With me in your company.

HERO I may say so when I please.   65

DON PEDRO And when please you to say so?

HERO When I like your favour, for God defend the lute should be like
the case.

DON PEDRO My visor is Philemon's roof, within the house is Jove.

HERO Why then your visor should be thatched.

DON PEDRO   Speak low if you speak love.   70

[*They move on in the dance*]

[BALTHASAR] Well, I would you did like me.

MARGARET So would not I for your own sake, for I have many ill
qualities.

[BALTHASAR] Which is one?

MARGARET I say my prayers aloud.   75

[BALTHASAR] I love you the better, the hearers may cry amen.

MARGARET God match me with a good dancer.

BALTHASAR Amen.

MARGARET And God keep him out of my sight when the dance is done:
answer, clerk.   80

BALTHASAR No more words, the clerk is answered.

[*They move on in the dance*]

URSULA I know you well enough, you are Signor Antonio.

ANTONIO At a word, I am not.

URSULA I know you by the waggling of your head.

ANTONIO To tell you true, I counterfeit him.   85

URSULA You could never do him so ill-well, unless you were the very
man: here's his dry hand up and down, you are he, you are he.

ANTONIO At a word, I am not.

URSULA Come, come, do you think I do not know you by your excellent
wit? Can virtue hide itself? Go to, mum, you are he, graces will   90
appear, and there's an end.

[*They move on in the dance*]

31

Benedick, believing his true identity to be hidden behind his mask, teases Beatrice, who promptly turns the tables on him. Don John and Borachio tell Claudio that Don Pedro loves Hero and intends to marry her.

1 Ouch!

Benedick momentarily lifts his mask so we can see how Beatrice's words have really stung him. Find the words you think she has just said to him.

2 Claudio pretends to be Benedick (in groups of three)

Claudio has no doubt been anxiously watching Don Pedro courting Hero. Rehearse lines 115–27 for presentation to the class. Show how Don John and Borachio seize this opportunity to trick the masked Claudio, and how he reacts, especially at line 124: 'How know you he loves her?'

The Hundred . . . Tales   a joke book
What's he?   Who's he?
only his gift   his only talent
libertines   good-for-nothings
villainy   offensiveness
angers them   i.e. when he makes offensive jokes about them

fleet   company
but . . . comparison   just make a few clever remarks
peradventure   perhaps
partridge wing   a small morsel
amorous on   in love with
visor   masked person

BEATRICE Will you not tell me who told you so?

BENEDICK No, you shall pardon me.

BEATRICE Nor will you not tell me who you are?

BENEDICK Not now.   95

BEATRICE That I was disdainful, and that I had my good wit out of *The
Hundred Merry Tales*: well, this was Signor Benedick that said so.

BENEDICK What's he?

BEATRICE I am sure you know him well enough.

BENEDICK Not I, believe me.   100

BEATRICE Did he never make you laugh? *Like a clown (not a very idiot good one).*

BENEDICK I pray you, what is he?

BEATRICE Why he is the prince's jester, a very dull fool, only his gift is, in
devising impossible slanders: none but libertines delight in him, and
the commendation is not in his wit, but in his villainy, for he both   105
pleases men and angers them, and then they laugh at him, and beat
him: I am sure he is in the fleet, I would he had boarded me.

BENEDICK When I know the gentleman, I'll tell him what you say.

BEATRICE Do, do, he'll but break a comparison or two on me, which
peradventure (not marked, or not laughed at) strikes him into   110
melancholy, and then there's a partridge wing saved, for the fool will
eat no supper that night. We must follow the leaders.

BENEDICK In every good thing.

BEATRICE Nay, if they lead to any ill, I will leave them at the next turning.
Music for the Dance. [*They Dance.*] *Exeunt* [*all but Don John,
Borachio and Claudio*]

DON JOHN Sure my brother is amorous on Hero, and hath withdrawn her 115
father to break with him about it: the ladies follow her, and but one
visor remains.

BORACHIO And that is Claudio, I know him by his bearing.

DON JOHN Are not you Signor Benedick?

CLAUDIO You know me well, I am he.   120

DON JOHN Signor, you are very near my brother in his love, he is
enamoured on Hero, I pray you dissuade him from her, she is no
equal for his birth: you may do the part of an honest man in it.

CLAUDIO How know you he loves her?

DON JOHN I heard him swear his affection.   125

BORACHIO So did I too, and he swore he would marry her tonight.

DON JOHN Come, let us to the banquet.
Exeunt Don John and Borachio

Claudio believes Don John's lie. Benedick also tells him that Don Pedro has won the heart of Hero. The unhappy Claudio creeps away, leaving Benedick smarting at the memory of Beatrice's taunting words.

1 Claudio reflects on events (in groups of about six)

Alone for a moment, Claudio reveals his inner thoughts in blank verse. Read his soliloquy together (lines 128–38), each person handing over to the next person at a colon or full stop. Try it in different ways: quickly and angrily, slowly and resignedly, full of anguish and despair. Decide which way works best and where Claudio places the blame – on Don Pedro or on Hero?

2 Claudio – a man or a mouse? (in pairs)

Benedick uses contrasting images to describe what Claudio must now do (lines 143–6):

- either give up Hero and wear the willow garland (the badge of the unhappy lover) round his neck like a money-lender's ('usurer's') gold chain
- or be a man, challenge the prince to a fight and wear the willow garland bravely across his chest like a soldier's sash.

Read lines 147–54 (to 'sedges') together and decide which option Claudio is likely to choose. Find three images that Benedick uses to describe his friend's reaction to losing Hero. What picture do they create of this brave young war hero?

3 Benedick reflects on events (in pairs)

Unlike Claudio, Benedick prefers to think in prose. See how he argues with himself (or with the audience?). Sit facing each other and read lines 154–9 aloud together. Change seats at each colon or exclamation mark. Decide how the argument changes and show that in your voice. How deeply have Beatrice's words hurt Benedick?

Afterwards, write detailed notes instructing an actor on how best to speak these six lines on stage.

---

faith loyalty (to a friend)
blood passion
accident . . . proof something which is constantly being proved true
mistrusted not did not suspect
county count

drovier cattle drover or dealer
served you treated you
sedges undergrowth
puts . . . person assumes the world thinks as she does
so gives me out causes such things to be said about me

[Handwritten annotation: Claudio speaks poetry / verse shows strong emotion, wants to be a hero]

CLAUDIO Thus answer I in name of Benedick,

But hear these ill news with the ears of Claudio:

'Tis certain so, the prince woos for himself,   130

Friendship is constant in all other things,

Save in the office and affairs of love:

Therefore all hearts in love use their own tongues.

Let every eye negotiate for itself, *[Blames Nero]*

And trust no agent: for beauty is a witch,   135

Against whose charms faith melteth into blood:

This is an accident of hourly proof,

Which I mistrusted not: farewell therefore, Hero.

[Handwritten annotation left margin: Makes Claudio seem like the ideal man]

[Handwritten annotation right margin: poetry]

Enter BENEDICK

[Handwritten annotation: ready to give up (Love is weak)]

BENEDICK Count Claudio. *[Being realistic]*

[Handwritten annotation: He wants to be a poetic lover]

CLAUDIO Yea, the same.   140

BENEDICK Come, will you go with me? *[Don Pedro is way more powerful]*

CLAUDIO Whither? *[conventional — because]*

BENEDICK Even to the next willow, about your own business, county:
what fashion will you wear the garland of? About your neck, like an
usurer's chain? Or under your arm, like a lieutenant's scarf? You   145
must wear it one way, for the prince hath got your Hero.

CLAUDIO I wish him joy of her. *[sarcastic, bitter, given up]*

BENEDICK Why that's spoken like an honest drovier, so they sell bull-
ocks: but did you think the prince would have served you thus?

CLAUDIO I pray you leave me.   150

BENEDICK Ho now you strike like the blind man, 'twas the boy that stole
your meat, and you'll beat the post.

CLAUDIO If it will not be, I'll leave you.   *Exit*

BENEDICK Alas poor hurt fowl, now will he creep into sedges: but that my
Lady Beatrice should know me, and not know me: the prince's fool!   155
Hah, it may be I go under that title because I am merry: yea but so I
am apt to do myself wrong: I am not so reputed, it is the base (though
bitter) disposition of Beatrice, that puts the world into her person,
and so gives me out: well, I'll be revenged as I may.

Benedick accuses Don Pedro of stealing Hero for himself, but the prince assures him that he has kept his promise to Claudio. Benedick angrily relates how cruelly Beatrice had insulted him during the dance.

1 A tricky situation for Benedick (in pairs)

Benedick genuinely believes that Don Pedro has taken Hero for himself. But how do you criticise the behaviour of a powerful prince?

Read lines 160–78. Talk about how Benedick uses humour (e.g. the image of schoolboys and a bird's nest) to soften the seriousness of his accusations. How happy is he with the prince's explanation (lines 177–8)?

2 Express Benedick's anger and frustration (in groups of about six)

We are close to the climax of the feud between Benedick and Beatrice. He describes her in lines 190–7:

- Beatrice renders men powerless, just as the queen of Lydia enslaved the mighty Hercules (see p. 183). In Beatrice's company Benedick feels like a man used as target practice ('at a mark') by an army of archers.
- Beatrice is Ate, the goddess of discord, who lived by the gates of hell. Benedick wants her 'conjured' back there. Men now sin deliberately ('upon purpose') just to be sent to hell and get out of Beatrice's way.

a Read aloud lines 181–97, handing over to the next person at each colon or full stop. Use a chair to represent Beatrice and direct your anger and frustration towards it, using both voice and gesture.

b List four phrases which create the best picture of this fearsome woman and decide which of Beatrice's taunts has hurt Benedick most of all.

Lady Fame   rumour
lodge . . . warren   lonely hut in a hunting park
flat transgression   simple offence
amiss   in vain
my very visor   even my mask
a great thaw   slush and mud after snow melts

impossible conveyance   unbelievable trickery
poniards   daggers
terminations   way she uses words
turned spit   turned the roasting spit
cleft   split

Enter DON PEDRO

DON PEDRO Now, signor, where's the count, did you see him?   160

BENEDICK Troth, my lord, I have played the part of Lady Fame, I found
    him here as melancholy as a lodge in a warren; I told him, and I think I
    told him true, that your grace had got the good will of this young lady,
    and I offered him my company to a willow tree, either to make him a
    garland, as being forsaken, or to bind him up a rod, as being worthy to   165
    be whipped.

DON PEDRO To be whipped: what's his fault?

BENEDICK The flat transgression of a schoolboy, who being overjoyed
    with finding a bird's nest, shows it his companion, and he steals it.

DON PEDRO Wilt thou make a trust a transgression? The transgression is   170
    in the stealer.

BENEDICK Yet it had not been amiss the rod had been made, and the
    garland too, for the garland he might have worn himself, and the rod
    he might have bestowed on you, who (as I take it) have stolen his
    bird's nest.   175

DON PEDRO I will but teach them to sing, and restore them to the owner.

BENEDICK If their singing answer your saying, by my faith, you say
    honestly.

DON PEDRO The Lady Beatrice hath a quarrel to you, the gentleman that
    danced with her told her she is much wronged by you.   180

BENEDICK Oh she misused me past the endurance of a block: an oak but
    with one green leaf on it, would have answered her: my very visor
    began to assume life, and scold with her: she told me, not thinking I
    had been myself, that I was the prince's jester, that I was duller than a
    great thaw, huddling jest upon jest, with such impossible conveyance   185
    upon me, that I stood like a man at a mark, with a whole army shooting
    at me: she speaks poniards, and every word stabs: if her breath were
    as terrible as her terminations, there were no living near her, she
    would infect to the north star: I would not marry her, though she were   190
    endowed with all that Adam had left him before he transgressed: she
    would have made Hercules have turned spit, yea, and have cleft his
    club to make the fire too: come, talk not of her, you shall find her the
    infernal Ate in good apparel. I would to God some scholar would
    conjure her, for certainly, while she is here, a man may live as quiet in
    hell, as in a sanctuary, and people sin upon purpose, because they   195
    would go thither, so indeed all disquiet, horror and perturbation
    follows her.

Benedick, in hugely extravagant fashion, leaves to avoid meeting Beatrice. She hints that they may have loved each other once. Don Pedro informs Claudio that he has won Hero's hand on Claudio's behalf.

1 A 'merry war' no longer (in groups of three)

Some productions have made this a comic yet painful moment by showing Beatrice overhearing much of what Benedick says in lines 199–208, as he asks Don Pedro to send him on impossibly point-less tasks just so he can avoid her company.

Try speaking lines 199–217 in different ways, to bring out the comedy, or the pain, or both. What do you imagine is going through the minds of Beatrice and Benedick?

2 How did the 'merry war' first start? (in small groups)

Sometimes an actor will prepare a role by imagining their character's life-history before the play. Shakespeare offers a tantalising glimpse of Beatrice and Benedick's 'pre-history' in lines 209–16. Talk about what clues might be in these lines and then write your story of how the Beatrice and Benedick feud began.

3 Show Claudio's discomfort (in groups of five)

Don Pedro and Leonato keep Claudio in suspense for a moment before revealing their surprise.

a Rehearse the betrothal scene (lines 216–40). Show Claudio's unhappiness and the secret amusement of Don Pedro and Leonato. Is Hero also happy?

b 'Civil, count, civil as an orange'. Beatrice (lines 222–4) puns on 'civil' and 'Seville'. A Seville orange is bitter-tasting and yellowish in colour. How apt a description of Claudio is this pun?

Antipodes opposite side of the world

tooth-picker a maker of toothpicks

Prester John legendary African king

Great Cham Mongol emperor

embassage errand

Harpy fierce bird-like monster with a beautiful female face

put . . . down humiliated (also 'get someone pregnant', as in Beatrice's reply)

blazon description

conceit belief

Enter CLAUDIO *and* BEATRICE, LEONATO [*and*] HERO

DON PEDRO Look, here she comes.

BENEDICK Will your grace command me any service to the world's end? I
will go on the slightest errand now to the Antipodes that you can   200
devise to send me on: I will fetch you a tooth-picker now from the
furthest inch of Asia: bring you the length of Prester John's foot: fetch
you a hair off the Great Cham's beard: do you any embassage to the
Pygmies, rather than hold three words conference with this Harpy:
you have no employment for me?   205

DON PEDRO None, but to desire your good company.

BENEDICK Oh God, sir, here's a dish I love not, I cannot endure my Lady
Tongue.   *Exit*

DON PEDRO Come, lady, come, you have lost the heart of Signor
Benedick.   210

BEATRICE Indeed, my lord, he lent it me a while, and I gave him use for it,
a double heart for his single one: marry once before he won it of me,
with false dice, therefore your grace may well say I have lost it.

DON PEDRO You have put him down, lady, you have put him down.

BEATRICE So I would not he should do me, my lord, lest I should prove   215
the mother of fools: I have brought Count Claudio, whom you sent
me to seek.

DON PEDRO Why how now, count, wherefore are you sad?

CLAUDIO Not sad, my lord.

DON PEDRO How then? Sick?   220

CLAUDIO Neither, my lord.

BEATRICE The count is neither sad, nor sick, nor merry, nor well: but
civil, count, civil as an orange, and something of that jealous
complexion.

DON PEDRO I'faith, lady, I think your blazon to be true, though I'll be   225
sworn, if he be so, his conceit is false: here, Claudio, I have wooed in
thy name, and fair Hero is won: I have broke with her father, and his
good will obtained: name the day of marriage, and God give thee joy.

Claudio and Hero are formally betrothed. When Beatrice jokingly complains that she is the only one left without a husband, Don Pedro offers himself as a candidate for Beatrice's hand in marriage, but she refuses.

1 A heart-warming betrothal? (in groups of five)

Read together lines 229–40. To help you understand who talks to whom, speak slowly and point to the correct character at every 'person' word (e.g. 'count', 'lady', 'cousin', and also words like 'my', 'he', 'his', 'you').

Then rehearse the lines with natural movements and actions (e.g. smiles, kisses, whispers). Present your version to the rest of the class. Give reasons why you think this will / will not be a lasting and happy marriage.

2 The lady and the prince (in pairs)

What exactly are Beatrice and Don Pedro up to in lines 241–55? Does Beatrice genuinely fish for a proposal from the prince? Does he seriously propose marriage? Take parts, then stand or sit face to face and speak your lines in the following ways:

- As Beatrice flirts with Don Pedro, he makes a light-hearted proposal, which she gently turns down.
- Don Pedro makes a serious proposal, which Beatrice politely rejects.
- Don Pedro makes a serious proposal, which Beatrice bluntly, almost cruelly, turns down.
- Beatrice's boldness in inviting a prince to propose to her offends Don Pedro and she quickly has to apologise.

Which version best fits with what you think these two personalities are like?

---

all grace God
dote upon love madly
on the windy side of away from (a sailing ship kept upwind to avoid attack)
alliance relatives (Claudio has just called her 'cousin')
goes . . . world gets married

sunburnt unattractive
getting offspring ('fathering')
no matter never seriously
out a question undoubtedly
star . . . born i.e. the dancing star influenced her personality
I cry you mercy forgive me

Hero → Represents marry for him like a business deal.

LEONATO Count, take of me my daughter, and with her my fortunes: his
    grace hath made the match, and all grace say amen to it.   230

BEATRICE Speak, count, 'tis your cue. *Only then claudio speaks to Hero*

CLAUDIO Silence is the perfectest herald of joy, I were but little happy if I
    could say, how much! Lady, as you are mine, I am yours: I give away
    myself for you, and dote upon the exchange.

BEATRICE Speak, cousin, or (if you cannot) stop his mouth with a kiss,   235
    and let not him speak neither.

DON PEDRO In faith, lady, you have a merry heart.

BEATRICE Yea, my lord, I thank it, poor fool it keeps on the windy side
    of care: my cousin tells him in his ear that he is in her heart.

CLAUDIO And so she doth, cousin.   240

BEATRICE Good Lord for alliance: thus goes every one to the world but I,
    and I am sunburnt, I may sit in a corner and cry, 'Heigh ho for a
    husband.'

DON PEDRO Lady Beatrice, I will get you one.

BEATRICE I would rather have one of your father's getting: hath your   245
    grace ne'er a brother like you? Your father got excellent husbands, if a
    maid could come by them.

DON PEDRO Will you have me, lady?

BEATRICE No, my lord, unless I might have another for working-days,
    your grace is too costly to wear every day: but I beseech your grace   250
    pardon me, I was born to speak all mirth, and no matter.

DON PEDRO Your silence most offends me, and to be merry, best
    becomes you, for out a question, you were born in a merry hour.

BEATRICE No sure, my lord, my mother cried, but then there was a star
    danced, and under that was I born: cousins, God give you joy.   255

LEONATO Niece, will you look to those things I told you of?

BEATRICE I cry you mercy, uncle: by your grace's pardon.   *Exit*

The marriage of Hero and Claudio is set for a week ahead. In the meantime, Don Pedro proposes some entertainment for them all. He has a plan to trick Beatrice and Benedick into falling in love with each other.

1 Is Beatrice really 'an excellent wife for Benedick'?

Look back over events so far and find as many serious reasons as you can for agreeing with Don Pedro. Then list as many reasons as you can for agreeing with Leonato's very doubtful response (lines 266–7).

2 'There's little of the melancholy element in her'

Many Elizabethans still held to the old belief that there were four humours (or fluids) in the human body. They gave rise to four basic types of personality, depending on which humour was predominant:

Melancholy (cold and dry)	cold, gloomy, depressed (melancholic)
Choler (hot and dry)	angry, quarrelsome, violent (choleric)
Phlegm (cool and moist)	cool, sluggish, apathetic (phlegmatic)
Blood (warm and moist)	warm, hopeful, confident (sanguine)

Assign each character in the play to their most appropriate 'humour'. You may well have differences in opinion here. Shakespeare's characters are rather more complex than the medieval system of humours!

3 Important moments from this scene (in groups of ten or more)

In the theatre this scene can be spectacular, full of colour, stage action, clever conversation, dancing and music (see page viii in the colour picture section and p. 32). Devise your own mime (or silent-film) version of the key moment, plus a narrative for one of you to speak to accompany your presentation. You could also make masks and select suitable music.

---

out of suit   out of pursuing her
rites   (1) religious rites of marriage
  (2) rights as a husband
a just seven-night   exactly a week
answer my mind   arranged as I want
  them
breathing   delay

Hercules' labours   (see p. 183)
fain   gladly
fashion it   make it happen
honesty   worth, honour
practise on   deceive, work on
queasy stomach   weak disposition
my drift   what I propose

DON PEDRO By my troth a pleasant spirited lady.

LEONATO There's little of the melancholy element in her, my lord, she is never sad, but when she sleeps, and not ever sad then: for I have heard my daughter say, she hath often dreamed of unhappiness, and waked herself with laughing.   260

DON PEDRO She cannot endure to hear tell of a husband.

LEONATO Oh by no means, she mocks all her wooers out of suit.

DON PEDRO She were an excellent wife for Benedick.   265

LEONATO Oh Lord, my lord, if they were but a week married, they would talk themselves mad.

DON PEDRO County Claudio, when mean you to go to church?

CLAUDIO Tomorrow, my lord: time goes on crutches, till love have all his rites.   270

LEONATO Not till Monday, my dear son, which is hence a just seven-night, and a time too brief too, to have all things answer my mind.

DON PEDRO Come, you shake the head at so long a breathing, but I warrant thee, Claudio, the time shall not go dully by us. I will in the interim undertake one of Hercules' labours, which is, to bring Signor   275 Benedick and the Lady Beatrice into a mountain of affection, th'one with th'other: I would fain have it a match, and I doubt not but to fashion it, if you three will but minister such assistance as I shall give you direction.

LEONATO My lord, I am for you, though it cost me ten nights' watchings.   280

CLAUDIO And I, my lord.

DON PEDRO And you too, gentle Hero?

HERO I will do any modest office, my lord, to help my cousin to a good husband.

DON PEDRO And Benedick is not the unhopefullest husband that I know: 285 thus far can I praise him, he is of a noble strain, of approved valour, and confirmed honesty. I will teach you how to humour your cousin, that she shall fall in love with Benedick, and I, with your two helps, will so practise on Benedick, that in despite of his quick wit, and his queasy stomach, he shall fall in love with Beatrice: if we can do this,   290 Cupid is no longer an archer, his glory shall be ours, for we are the only love-gods. Go in with me, and I will tell you my drift.

Exeunt

Don John's first plot against Claudio has failed. Borachio now proposes a much more dishonest scheme which will convince Claudio and Don Pedro that Hero is having an affair with another man.

1 The sky begins to darken (in small groups)

Beatrice and Benedick's friends are planning some innocent amusement at their expense. Don John and Borachio have a more unpleasant aim – to ruin Hero's honour.

a **Evil and villainy** Two of you read this scene aloud. The rest repeat or echo all the 'evil' or 'villainous' words that are spoken. Decide which of the two men is the greater villain, and why.

b **Images of disease and death** Find four sickness/death words that Don John and Borachio use as they discuss their plan.

2 The villains intervene, but where and when?

Neither the time nor the setting for this scene were made clear in early editions of the play. It could be inside Leonato's house, in his garden, or outside in the street. Neither is it clear whether the action follows on immediately from the end of Scene 1, or whether some time has elapsed.

Read the final lines of the previous scene (lines 287–92) together with the opening lines of this scene (lines 1–10). Decide where and when you think this new scene should be set. Write down the reasons for your decision.

---

cross it prevent it
medicinable to me make me feel well
comes . . . affection frustrates his desires
ranges . . . mine satisfies me
covertly secretly
unseasonable inappropriate

temper mix, concoct
whose estimation . . . hold up whose honour you most strongly proclaim
contaminated stale diseased prostitute
misuse deceive
issue outcome

Act 2 Scene 2
Leonato's house

Enter DON JOHN and BORACHIO

DON JOHN It is so, the Count Claudio shall marry the daughter of
Leonato.

BORACHIO Yea, my lord, but I can cross it.

DON JOHN Any bar, any cross, any impediment, will be medicinable to
me, I am sick in displeasure to him, and whatsoever comes athwart his   5
affection, ranges evenly with mine. How canst thou cross this
marriage?

BORACHIO Not honestly, my lord, but so covertly, that no dishonesty
shall appear in me.

DON JOHN Show me briefly how.   10

BORACHIO I think I told your lordship a year since, how much I am in the
favour of Margaret, the waiting gentlewoman to Hero.

DON JOHN I remember.

BORACHIO I can at any unseasonable instant of the night, appoint her to
look out at her lady's chamber window.   15

DON JOHN What life is in that to be the death of this marriage?

BORACHIO The poison of that lies in you to temper; go you to the prince
your brother, spare not to tell him, that he hath wronged his honour in
marrying the renowned Claudio, whose estimation do you mightily
hold up, to a contaminated stale, such a one as Hero.   20

DON JOHN What proof shall I make of that?

BORACHIO Proof enough, to misuse the prince, to vex Claudio, to undo
Hero, and kill Leonato; look you for any other issue?

DON JOHN Only to despite them I will endeavour anything.

Borachio's plan is that he and Margaret will appear on the night before the wedding at Hero's bedroom window. They will call each other Hero and Claudio, so deceiving the watching Don Pedro and Claudio.

Borachio outlines a plan that will 'undo Hero, and kill Leonato'.

1 Honour, reputation and virginity

Count the number of times these three virtues are mentioned in this scene. People have so far talked of such matters with casual and light-hearted confidence. Borachio's plan, with its talk of 'semblance' (outward show) and 'seeming truth', will test each character's moral soundness to the very limit.

meet   suitable
intend   pretend you have
zeal   earnestness
as in love of   as if you were concerned for
like to be   about to be
cozened with   duped by

the semblance of a maid   a woman who only seems a virgin
trial   proof, evidence
likelihood   plausibility
jealousy . . . assurance   mere suspicion will become certainty
ducats   Italian silver coins

BORACHIO Go then, find me a meet hour to draw Don Pedro and the   25
    Count Claudio alone, tell them that you know that Hero loves me,
    intend a kind of zeal both to the prince and Claudio (as in love of your
    brother's honour who hath made this match, and his friend's repu-
    tation, who is thus like to be cozened with the semblance of a maid)
    that you have discovered thus: they will scarcely believe this without   30
    trial: offer them instances which shall bear no less likelihood, than to
    see me at her chamber window, hear me call Margaret Hero, hear
    Margaret term me Claudio, and bring them to see this the very night
    before the intended wedding, for in the mean time, I will so fashion
    the matter, that Hero shall be absent, and there shall appear such   35
    seeming truth of Hero's disloyalty, that jealousy shall be called
    assurance, and all the preparation overthrown.
DON JOHN Grow this to what adverse issue it can, I will put it in practice:
    be cunning in the working this, and thy fee is a thousand ducats.
BORACHIO Be you constant in the accusation, and my cunning shall not   40
    shame me.
DON JOHN I will presently go learn their day of marriage.

Exeunt

Benedick muses on men like Claudio who say they will not fall in love and then do so. He lists the many virtues he would require in a future wife. When the prince, Claudio and Leonato approach, Benedick hides.

1 When does the boy return?

The script does not tell us! Some productions have set up a running joke as the boy chases through scene after scene vainly attempting to deliver Benedick's book. After reading through this scene, decide where the boy might most amusingly attempt to give Benedick his book.

2 Benedick's exasperation with Claudio (in groups of three)

Benedick (lines 7–17) can scarcely believe the change in his friend's behaviour from soldier to lovesick swain. One of you takes the role of Claudio as he used to be, another plays him as he is now. The third person is Benedick, who exasperatedly introduces the two Claudios to the class and tells the whole sorry story. Use your own words and/or words from the script.

3 A very smug Benedick? (in pairs)

In lines 18–21 Benedick wonders if one day he too might fall in love, then quickly dismisses the idea. Try the following activity to help you show the balanced patterns in his sentences which help convey a complacent confidence that he is immune to love's power.

Speak lines 21–7, sharing out the sentence parts so as to highlight the balances and contrasts (e.g. one says 'one woman is fair' and the other 'yet I am well'). Show your 'twin-Benedick' to the class. Remember to speak in a smugly self-satisfied way.

---

am . . . already   will do it at once (Benedick takes him literally)
argument   object
drum . . . fife   music of war
tabor . . . pipe   music of peace
carving   designing
doublet   close-fitting waistcoat

turned orthography   speaking an elaborate, flowery language
oyster   i.e. shut up in moody silence
well   not ill with love
come in my grace   get my approval
cheapen   make an offer for
noble/angel   names of coins

Act 2 Scene 3
Leonato's orchard

Enter BENEDICK *alone*

BENEDICK Boy.

BOY [*within*] Signor.

[*Enter* BOY]

BENEDICK In my chamber window lies a book, bring it hither to me in
the orchard.

BOY I am here already, sir.   5

BENEDICK I know that, but I would have thee hence and here again.

Exit [*Boy*]

I do much wonder, that one man seeing how much another man is a
fool, when he dedicates his behaviours to love, will after he hath
laughed at such shallow follies in others, become the argument of
his own scorn, by falling in love: and such a man is Claudio. I have   10
known when there was no music with him but the drum and the fife,
and now had he rather hear the tabor and the pipe: I have known
when he would have walked ten mile afoot, to see a good armour,
and now will he lie ten nights awake carving the fashion of a new
doublet: he was wont to speak plain and to the purpose (like an   15
honest man and a soldier) and now is he turned orthography, his
words are a very fantastical banquet, just so many strange dishes:
may I be so converted and see with these eyes? I cannot tell, I think
not: I will not be sworn but love may transform me to an oyster, but
I'll take my oath on it, till he have made an oyster of me, he shall   20
never make me such a fool: one woman is fair, yet I am well: another
is wise, yet I am well: another virtuous, yet I am well: but till all
graces be in one woman, one woman shall not come in my grace:
rich she shall be, that's certain: wise, or I'll none: virtuous, or I'll
never cheapen her: fair, or I'll never look on her: mild, or come not   25
near me: noble, or not I for an angel: of good discourse, an excellent
musician – and her hair shall be of what colour it please God. Hah!
the prince and Monsieur Love, I will hide me in the arbour.

Don Pedro, Claudio and Leonato pretend not to notice the hidden Benedick. They prepare to listen to Balthasar's singing. Benedick is not impressed by the romantic music.

1 Where does Benedick hide? (in small groups)

Look at the picture on page ix (top) in the colour section to see where one Benedick tried to hide himself. Another Benedick hid inside a tree (see p. 54). He loved to smoke cigars, so puffs of smoke rose from inside the tree as he listened to his friends' conversation.

Choose a place in your school or college grounds that would be suitable for an open-air production of *Much Ado About Nothing*. Decide where you could most originally or amusingly hide Benedick. Remember that he will need to be both heard and seen by the audience.

2 Benedick's poetic friends

Knowing Benedick is hidden nearby, the prince and his friends speak poetic blank verse as befits the love-obsessed characters they are pretending to be (lines 30–49).

a Write down your favourite romantic line/phrase plus any lines which you think are decidedly unromantic. Give reasons for your choices.

b The unromantic Benedick interrupts in prose when Balthasar is about to sing (line 50), saying 'now is his soul ravished [overcome with pleasure]'. Who might he be referring to and what could that actor have done to prompt Benedick's sardonic outburst?

3 Nothing and noting again (in pairs)

Take a part each and read aloud lines 44–9. Practise saying these lines in a way that highlights the wordplay on 'notes', 'noting', 'nothing'. Compare this exchange with Act 1 Scene 1, lines 119–20. What extra meaning does Balthasar give to the word 'note'?

---

fit . . . pennyworth   give Benedick more than he bargains for
tax not   do not order
slander   bring disgrace on
witness still   always a sign
put . . . face on   pretend not to recognise

suit   courtship
Do it in notes   be brief
crotchets   (1) fanciful ideas (2) notes in music
sheep's guts   strings of a lute
hale   draw, fetch
horn   military trumpet

Enter DON PEDRO, LEONATO, CLAUDIO [*and* BALTHASAR *with*] *music*

DON PEDRO Come, shall we hear this music?

CLAUDIO Yea, my good lord: how still the evening is,   30
    As hushed on purpose to grace harmony!

DON PEDRO See you where Benedick hath hid himself?

CLAUDIO Oh very well, my lord: the music ended,
    We'll fit the kid-fox with a pennyworth.

DON PEDRO Come, Balthasar, we'll hear that song again.   35

BALTHASAR Oh, good my lord, tax not so bad a voice,
    To slander music any more than once.

DON PEDRO It is the witness still of excellency,
    To put a strange face on his own perfection:
    I pray thee sing, and let me woo no more.   40

BALTHASAR Because you talk of wooing I will sing,
    Since many a wooer doth commence his suit,
    To her he thinks not worthy, yet he woos,
    Yet will he swear he loves.

DON PEDRO   Nay, pray thee come,
    Or if thou wilt hold longer argument,   45
    Do it in notes.

BALTHASAR   Note this before my notes,
    There's not a note of mine that's worth the noting.

DON PEDRO Why these are very crotchets that he speaks,
    Note notes forsooth, and nothing.

                       [*Music*]

BENEDICK Now divine air, now is his soul ravished: is it not strange that   50
sheep's guts should hale souls out of men's bodies? Well, a horn for
my money when all's done.

Balthasar sings his song about the fickleness of men. He is sent by Don Pedro to prepare the music that will be used to serenade Hero at her chamber window the next night.

___

1 'Sigh no more, ladies, sigh no more' (in small groups)

Shakespeare often uses music and song in his plays, always with the purpose of intensifying dramatic effect. But why should he put a song here just when the audience wants to see how Benedick will be fooled? Try some or all of the following:

a **Men are faithless and deceitful** Deception is a major preoccupation of the play. Speak the song, taking a line each. Which lines echo this theme and how will Benedick, Claudio, Don Pedro and Leonato all be deceived? List the many examples of deception practised so far in the play. Have they all been perpetrated by men?

b **Sing the song!** Compose an appropriate tune for this song. One of you sing the first verse while the others listen in role as one of the characters. Then all of you sing the second verse together. Talk about the emotions your song evokes.

c **Is the song sung well?** Decide how impressed Don Pedro and Benedick are with Balthasar's singing (lines 69–75). If you were producing the play, would you have the song sung well or badly? Talk about:
  • the effect of a movingly beautiful song heard at this moment
  • the comic effect that bad singing would create.

Pool your ideas and give at least four reasons why Shakespeare included lines 29–80.

___

blithe and bonny cheerful and carefree
hey nonny nonny (nonsense phrase)
no mo no more
dumps sadness, sad songs
fraud faithlessness
leavy full of leaves, 'leaf-y'

for a shift for want of a better
And he if he
bode foretells
as lief rather
night-raven its harsh cry foretold death or sickness

The Song

[BALTHASAR] Sigh no more, ladies, sigh no more,
    Men were deceivers ever,
One foot in sea, and one on shore,   55
    To one thing constant never.
Then sigh not so, but let them go,
    And be you blithe and bonny,
Converting all your sounds of woe,
    Into hey nonny nonny.   60

Sing no more ditties, sing no mo,
    Of dumps so dull and heavy,
The fraud of men was ever so,
    Since summer first was leavy.
Then sigh not so, but let them go,   65
    And be you blithe and bonny,
Converting all your sounds of woe,
    Into hey nonny nonny.

DON PEDRO By my troth a good song.

BALTHASAR And an ill singer, my lord.   70

DON PEDRO Ha, no no faith, thou sing'st well enough for a shift.

BENEDICK And he had been a dog that should have howled thus, they
    would have hanged him; and I pray God his bad voice bode no
    mischief, I had as lief have heard the night-raven, come what plague
    could have come after it.   75

DON PEDRO Yea marry, dost thou hear, Balthasar? I pray thee get us
    some excellent music: for tomorrow night we would have it at the
    Lady Hero's chamber window.

BALTHASAR The best I can, my lord.

DON PEDRO Do so, farewell.   80

Exit Balthasar

Don Pedro and the others begin their deception of Benedick. They talk about how Beatrice is madly in love with Benedick, but is too frightened to tell him of her secret passion.

1 The fooling of Benedick (in groups of five)

The trick ('gull') Benedick's friends play on him makes marvellous theatre. To get a first impression, and to see if their plot works, read through lines 81–213. Then explore Benedick's reactions.

The 1990 Royal Shakespeare Company production had Benedick hiding in a tree and peering through the foliage. He puffed smoke from his cigar, coughed, choked, and at one point fell out of the tree!

Prepare your version of lines 81–180. Show the enjoyment of Benedick's friends as they set about their plan. Which lines do the plotters whisper to themselves and which do they say deliberately loudly for Benedick's benefit?

Work out how to 'hide' Benedick so that your audience can still see his reactions (surprise, anger, pleasure, curiosity, hurt?). One production had him grab a pair of shears and pretend to be a gardener clipping a hedge (see p. ix (top)).

Show your version to the rest of the class.

---

stalk on . . . sits start your hunting, the game bird has settled

Sits . . . corner? Is that really the way things are?

it . . . thought it is unbelievable, but true

counterfeit pretend

near . . . passion close to real passion

discovers it shows it

gull trick

knavery villainy

hold it up keep it going

smock slip, undergarment

Come hither, Leonato, what was it you told me of today, that your niece Beatrice was in love with Signor Benedick?

CLAUDIO Oh aye, stalk on, stalk on, the fowl sits. I did never think that lady would have loved any man.

LEONATO No nor I neither, but most wonderful, that she should so dote 85 on Signor Benedick, whom she hath in all outward behaviours seemed ever to abhor.

BENEDICK Is't possible? Sits the wind in that corner?

LEONATO By my troth, my lord, I cannot tell what to think of it, but that she loves him with an enraged affection, it is past the infinite of 90 thought.

DON PEDRO May be she doth but counterfeit.

CLAUDIO Faith like enough.

LEONATO Oh God! Counterfeit? There was never counterfeit of passion, came so near the life of passion as she discovers it. 95

DON PEDRO Why what effects of passion shows she?

CLAUDIO Bait the hook well, this fish will bite.

LEONATO What effects, my lord? She will sit you – you heard my daughter tell you how.

CLAUDIO She did indeed. 100

DON PEDRO How, how, I pray you! You amaze me, I would have thought her spirit had been invincible against all assaults of affection.

LEONATO I would have sworn it had, my lord, especially against Benedick. 105

BENEDICK I should think this a gull, but that the white-bearded fellow speaks it: knavery cannot sure hide himself in such reverence.

CLAUDIO He hath ta'en th'infection, hold it up.

DON PEDRO Hath she made her affection known to Benedick?

LEONATO No, and swears she never will, that's her torment. 110

CLAUDIO 'Tis true indeed, so your daughter says: shall I, says she, that have so oft encountered him with scorn, write to him that I love him?

LEONATO This says she now when she is beginning to write to him, for she'll be up twenty times a night, and there will she sit in her smock, 115 till she have writ a sheet of paper: my daughter tells us all.

Don Pedro and the others talk about Beatrice's many fine qualities. They express their fear that Benedick will mock her if he learns of her great love for him.

1 Give it all you've got! (in groups of four)

The plan is going well and Benedick's three friends are enjoying themselves.

Take a part each (the fourth person is the listening Benedick) and read lines 122–59 at least twice. Express your concern for Beatrice and angry outrage at Benedick and his faults. Ask Benedick which comments about him hit home the hardest.

In the very first scene, Benedick admitted that Beatrice would be a beautiful woman if only 'she were not possessed with a fury' (Act 1 Scene 1, line 141). How do the three men convince Benedick that Beatrice is madly in love with him, and how do they persuade him to fall in love with her (lines 85–154)?

2 Lay it on with a trowel (in pairs)

The list is one of Shakespeare's favourite language techniques. In lines 126–8 he has Claudio go comically over the top describing Beatrice's lovesick misery. One of you slowly reads the list while the other melodramatically mimes each symptom of Beatrice's torment.

3 'I would she had bestowed this dotage on me'

Don Pedro has already asked Beatrice to marry him (Act 2 Scene 1, lines 241–8). Do you think he was serious then? Is he serious in lines 144–5 when he says that he wishes Beatrice were in love with him? If the prince were played as genuinely being in love with Beatrice, how would that affect your perception of his character and hers?

---

sheet   (1) paper (2) bed linen
flout   mock, ridicule
ecstasy   frenzy, passion
by some other   from someone else
discover it   reveal it
And he should   if he did
alms   a good deed

out of all suspicion   without doubt
blood   passion
dotage   passion
daffed . . . respects   put aside all other considerations
bate   give up, abate
tender   an offer

CLAUDIO Now you talk of a sheet of paper, I remember a pretty jest
your daughter told us of.

LEONATO Oh when she had writ it, and was reading it over, she found
Benedick and Beatrice between the sheet. 120

CLAUDIO That.

LEONATO Oh she tore the letter into a thousand halfpence, railed at
herself, that she should be so immodest to write to one that she
knew would flout her: I measure him, says she, by my own spirit, for
I should flout him, if he writ to me, yea, though I love him I should. 125

CLAUDIO Then down upon her knees she falls, weeps, sobs, beats her
heart, tears her hair, prays, curses, Oh sweet Benedick, God give
me patience.

LEONATO She doth indeed, my daughter says so, and the ecstasy hath
so much overborn her, that my daughter is sometime afeared she 130
will do a desperate outrage to herself, it is very true.

DON PEDRO It were good that Benedick knew of it by some other, if she
will not discover it.

CLAUDIO To what end? He would make but a sport of it, and torment
the poor lady worse. 135

DON PEDRO And he should, it were an alms to hang him: she's an
excellent sweet lady, and (out of all suspicion) she is virtuous.

CLAUDIO And she is exceeding wise.

DON PEDRO In everything but in loving Benedick.

LEONATO Oh my lord, wisdom and blood combating in so tender a 140
body, we have ten proofs to one, that blood hath the victory: I am
sorry for her, as I have just cause, being her uncle, and her
guardian.

DON PEDRO I would she had bestowed this dotage on me, I would have
daffed all other respects, and made her half myself: I pray you tell 145
Benedick of it, and hear what a will say.

LEONATO Were it good, think you?

CLAUDIO Hero thinks surely she will die, for she says she will die, if he
love her not, and she will die ere she make her love known, and she
will die if he woo her, rather than she will bate one breath of her 150
accustomed crossness.

DON PEDRO She doth well: if she should make tender of her love, 'tis
very possible he'll scorn it, for the man (as you know all) hath a
contemptible spirit.

Don Pedro, Claudio and Leonato leave, hoping they have completed their deception of Benedick. Don Pedro orders a similar trick to be played on Beatrice by Hero and her attendant gentlewomen.

---

1 I'll kill him!

Don Pedro is particularly enthusiastic in his abuse of Benedick (lines 155–67). Each time the others compliment Benedick, the prince turns it into a criticism. One hidden Benedick could barely restrain himself from breaking cover and punching the living daylights out of him! Decide which insult makes Benedick most angry and why.

This is how one actor showed Benedick's reaction to what he overheard. He is amazed, but completely convinced!

Before turning over to read what Benedick says, think of four reasons he might have for believing what his friends have 'revealed'.

---

proper handsome
outward happiness pleasing outward appearance
wit intelligence, wisdom
valiant brave
Hector Trojan warrior hero
a must he must

howsoever even though
by . . . jests . . . make judging by some of the rude jokes he tells
wear . . . counsel bear it with good sense
another's dotage the other's passion
no such matter completely untrue

CLAUDIO He is a very proper man.   155

DON PEDRO He hath indeed a good outward happiness.

CLAUDIO Before God, and in my mind, very wise.

DON PEDRO He doth indeed show some sparks that are like wit.

LEONATO And I take him to be valiant.

DON PEDRO As Hector, I assure you, and in the managing of quarrels   160
    you may say he is wise, for either he avoids them with great discre-
    tion, or undertakes them with a most christianlike fear.

LEONATO If he do fear God, a must necessarily keep peace: if he break
    the peace, he ought to enter into a quarrel with fear and trembling.

DON PEDRO And so will he do, for the man doth fear God, howsoever it   165
    seems not in him, by some large jests he will make: well, I am sorry
    for your niece: shall we go seek Benedick, and tell him of her love?

CLAUDIO Never tell him, my lord, let her wear it out with good counsel.

LEONATO Nay that's impossible, she may wear her heart out first.

DON PEDRO Well, we will hear further of it by your daughter, let it cool   170
    the while: I love Benedick well, and I could wish he would modestly
    examine himself, to see how much he is unworthy so good a lady.

LEONATO My lord, will you walk? Dinner is ready.

CLAUDIO If he do not dote on her upon this, I will never trust my
    expectation.   175

DON PEDRO Let there be the same net spread for her, and that must
    your daughter and her gentlewomen carry: the sport will be, when
    they hold one an opinion of another's dotage, and no such matter:
    that's the scene that I would see, which will be merely a dumb show:
    let us send her to call him in to dinner.   180

                                    [*Exeunt all but Benedick*]

Benedick is convinced that Beatrice loves him and resolves to return her affection. When she reluctantly appears to call him to dinner, he looks for some sign of love in her and amazingly finds one!

1 Benedick swallows the bait (in small groups)

Some actors speak Benedick's soliloquy (lines 181–200) as if trying to rationalise their sudden commitment to Beatrice. Others seem bewildered, or react with barely concealed delight. Explore the many possibilities.

- **'This can be no trick'** Speak Benedick's opening five words to the others in different ways (e.g. with delight, smug self-satisfaction, horror or solemn certainty).
- **'I hear how I am censured'** Take turns to read lines 184–8 (to 'mending'). How mature and honest is Benedick's response to his friends' criticisms?
- **'They say the lady is fair'** Beatrice suddenly seems a most desirable woman. Read lines 188–92 (to 'horribly in love with her'), changing speaker at each punctuation mark. Convince the others of Beatrice's virtues.
- **'I may chance have . . .'** Benedick realises he will now be the butt of many jokes. Read lines 192–8 (to 'till I were married'). Choose one of his defence arguments and attempt to convince your group.

Now read the whole soliloquy (lines 181–200), taking a sentence each. Which of Benedick's remarks do you think the audience will find the funniest?

2 The new Benedick meets the old Beatrice (in pairs)

The last time they met, Benedick called Beatrice a 'Harpy' (see p. 38). You can imagine the mood she is in when she is sent to collect him. But Benedick is a changed man! Speak lines 198–207 (from 'here comes Beatrice . . .') and let Beatrice tear shreds off the smiling lovesick Benedick (see also p. 62).

---

the conference was sadly borne the conversation was serious
have . . . bent are stretched to their limit (like a bow)
requited returned
censured judged
detractions faults, deficiencies
reprove deny

meat food
sentences witty sayings
awe frighten
career course
humour inclination
daw withal jackdaw with it
stomach appetite (for a fight)
Jew faithless rogue (see p. 187)

BENEDICK This can be no trick, the conference was sadly borne, they
have the truth of this from Hero, they seem to pity the lady: it seems
her affections have their full bent: love me? Why, it must be
requited: I hear how I am censured, they say I will bear myself
proudly, if I perceive the love come from her: they say too, that she   185
will rather die than give any sign of affection: I did never think to
marry, I must not seem proud, happy are they that hear their detractions, and can put them to mending: they say the lady is fair, 'tis a
truth, I can bear them witness: and virtuous, 'tis so, I cannot reprove
it: and wise, but for loving me: by my troth it is no addition to her   190
wit, nor no great argument of her folly, for I will be horribly in love
with her: I may chance have some odd quirks and remnants of wit
broken on me, because I have railed so long against marriage: but
doth not the appetite alter? A man loves the meat in his youth, that
he cannot endure in his age. Shall quips and sentences, and these   195
paper bullets of the brain awe a man from the career of his humour?
No, the world must be peopled. When I said I would die a bachelor,
I did not think I should live till I were married – here comes
Beatrice: by this day, she's a fair lady, I do spy some marks of love in
her.   200

Enter BEATRICE

BEATRICE Against my will I am sent to bid you come in to dinner.
BENEDICK Fair Beatrice, I thank you for your pains.
BEATRICE I took no more pains for those thanks, than you took pains to
thank me, if it had been painful I would not have come.
BENEDICK You take pleasure then in the message.   205
BEATRICE Yea, just so much as you may take upon a knife's point, and
choke a daw withal: you have no stomach, signor, fare you well. *Exit*
BENEDICK Ha, against my will I am sent to bid you come in to dinner:
there's a double meaning in that: I took no more pains for those
thanks than you took pains to thank me: that's as much as to say, any   210
pains that I take for you is as easy as thanks: if I do not take pity of
her I am a villain, if I do not love her I am a Jew, I will go get her
picture.   *Exit*

Looking back at Act 2
Activities for groups or individuals

1 Tell the story using your favourite lines and moments

Look back through Act 2 and write down selected lines and episodes that appeal to you. Get into a group and share your selections. Then put together your version of the events in this act using some or all of your favourite lines and moments plus your own words. Present it to the class.

2 Your thoughts on Hero and Claudio

Look back at what these young lovers say and do in Act 2. Talk about their personal qualities and how much they know about each other. Decide why they might behave as they do.

3 Your thoughts on Beatrice and Benedick

This Beatrice called Benedick into supper by banging the dinner gong very loudly in his ear. What line do you think Benedick is speaking?

Beatrice seems victorious in the battle of wits (Act 2 Scene 1, lines 103–7) when she calls Benedick 'the prince's jester'. She may feel less happy when Benedick later retaliates, branding her a 'Harpy'

(Act 2 Scene 1, lines 201–5). In pairs, devise two tableaux ('frozen moments') which show the feelings of Beatrice and Benedick at these two points in the play.

Look back at Benedick's reaction on overhearing that Beatrice is secretly in love with him (Act 2 Scene 3, lines 181–213). Write a short paragraph listing the admirable husband-like qualities he reveals. Explain why he was so easily duped by his friends.

Look back at Beatrice's comment in Act 2 Scene 1, lines 211–17. Explain why she may not be so easy to deceive.

4 Plots and patterns

Two pairs of lovers, two pairs of brothers, two conventional lovers, two unconventional lovers, two male friends, two female friends, two benevolent plots, two malevolent plots . . . and more!

Oppositions and patterns in the play are becoming clearer. Write down as many pairings as you can. Who belongs in which pair? Remember that the same character can appear in more than one pairing. For example, Claudio can be paired both as a friend and as a lover.

5 Slapstick trickery and other kinds of comedy

Choose your favourite moments and lines from the tricking of Benedick (Act 2 Scene 3). Using these lines, make up a high-speed two-minute slapstick (knockabout) version which highlights Benedick's change from avowed bachelor to a man 'horribly in love'.

Find as many kinds of verbal and visual humour as you can in Act 2. Look for witty or bitter wordplay, comic insults, sexual innuendoes and embarrassing situations, as well as further slapstick comedy possibilities (in one production, when Beatrice stormed off the dance floor, Benedick was reduced to grabbing a small child for a partner).

Then devise a group presentation of these comic moments. At the end, ask your audience to identify the different sorts of humour in your sketches.

6 Much ado about virginity?

The play's title has at least two meanings: 'nothing' and 'noting' (see pp. 10 and 50). Some people detect a third meaning: 'Much ado about virginity', because 'thing' in Elizabethan slang meant the female genitalia (nothing = no-thing). Do you think Act 2 can be used to justify this interpretation?

Hero begins her plan to trick Beatrice. Margaret is sent to tell Beatrice that
Hero and Ursula are in the orchard talking about her. Beatrice steals in to
eavesdrop on their conversation.

1 Find out how Beatrice is deceived (in pairs)

As Hero and Ursula, quickly read through lines 1–106 (ignore
Margaret's one line) and see if the trick is played on Beatrice as you
imagined it would be. Compare the women's tactics to those used by
the men in the previous scene.

2 A newly confident Hero (in groups of three)

In this scene the quiet, dutiful Hero suddenly blossoms. Take it in
turns to be Hero. The space around you is the orchard. In the distance
is the house where Beatrice and the men are. As Hero slowly reads
lines 1–25, she must point clearly to every place and person mentioned.
For example:

> Good Margaret (*point to Margaret*), run thee (*point again to Margaret*)
> to the parlour (*point to door*),
> There shalt thou (*point to Margaret*) find my (*point to self*) cousin
> Beatrice

Now rehearse this section with Hero sounding very much in charge.
Talk about the reasons for her sudden change of character.

3 'Like favourites,
Made proud by princes'

Using an unexpectedly political image, the newly assertive Hero compares the honeysuckle to favoured noblemen who grow too proud and
threaten to overwhelm their prince (lines 9–11). How relevant do you
think this simile is to the play? Decide which character it describes
most accurately.

Proposing talking
Ursley Ursula
discourse conversation
pleachèd bower shelter of interwoven
  branches
favourites favoured courtiers
that power i.e. the power of the
  princes

propose conversation
office task
presently straightaway
trace walk
crafty skilfully made, or cunning
by hearsay with words
like a lapwing (see p. 66)

Act 3 Scene 1
The orchard

Enter HERO *and two gentlewomen,* MARGARET *and* URSULA

HERO Good Margaret, run thee to the parlour,
       There shalt thou find my cousin Beatrice,
       Proposing with the prince and Claudio,
       Whisper her ear and tell her I and Ursley
       Walk in the orchard, and our whole discourse   5
       Is all of her, say that thou overheard'st us,
       And bid her steal into the pleachèd bower,
       Where honeysuckles ripened by the sun,
       Forbid the sun to enter: like favourites,
       Made proud by princes, that advance their pride,   10
       Against that power that bred it: there will she hide her,
       To listen our propose: this is thy office,
       Bear thee well in it, and leave us alone.
MARGARET I'll make her come I warrant you, presently.   *Exit*
HERO Now, Ursula, when Beatrice doth come,   15
       As we do trace this alley up and down,
       Our talk must only be of Benedick:
       When I do name him, let it be thy part,
       To praise him more than ever man did merit:
       My talk to thee must be how Benedick   20
       Is sick in love with Beatrice: of this matter
       Is little Cupid's crafty arrow made,
       That only wounds by hearsay: now begin,

Enter BEATRICE

       For look where Beatrice like a lapwing runs
       Close by the ground, to hear our conference.   25

Beatrice, thinking herself unobserved, listens in on Hero and Ursula's conversation. They talk of Benedick's 'love' for Beatrice and Hero expresses concern about Beatrice's proud and scornful nature.

1 Comic trickery or painful truth? (in groups of three)

The men spoke largely in lively prose, a more natural medium for a comic 'gulling'. These women, however, speak entirely in verse as if love were too serious a matter for riotous comedy. Some productions therefore create a more serious mood by 'hiding' Beatrice in full view of the audience, who can see every painful response to her friends' criticism (see page ix (bottom) in the colour section and p. 98).

Present your version of lines 26–58 to the rest of the class. Stage it so that Beatrice's face and reactions can be seen by the audience. Show her by turns shocked, guilty, puzzled, dismayed, angry and delighted. Talk about whether this 'gulling' should be entirely serious or at least partly humorous.

2 Images of Beatrice

In lines 24–5 Hero compares Beatrice to a lapwing, a bird which searches for food by running along close to the ground, stopping and leaning forward to look for insects, before running on again. What does this suggest about the way Beatrice reaches her hiding place?

In lines 35–6 Hero says that Beatrice's spirits are 'as coy [disdainful] and wild, / As haggards of the rock'. A 'haggard' is a wild female hawk, which is far more difficult to train than one reared in captivity. How does this comparison help you to understand Beatrice's behaviour in the play so far?

Find another 'creature image' used to describe Beatrice in lines 24–36. Does this comparison suggest that she will be easy or difficult to trick? (You will find more about imagery on pp. 182–3.)

---

couchèd   hidden
coverture   shelter
trothèd   engaged, betrothed
entreat   beg
wish him wrestle with   get him to fight
  against
couch   lie

framed   fashioned, shaped
Misprising   despising
wit   intelligence
seems weak   seems boring
take . . . affection   take on any
  appearance or notion of love
self-endeared   full of herself

URSULA   The pleasant'st angling is to see the fish
   Cut with her golden oars the silver stream,
   And greedily devour the treacherous bait:
   So angle we for Beatrice, who even now,
   Is couchèd in the woodbine coverture: 30
   Fear you not my part of the dialogue.
HERO   Then go we near her, that her ear lose nothing
   Of the false sweet bait that we lay for it:
   No truly, Ursula, she is too disdainful,
   I know her spirits are as coy and wild,   35
   As haggards of the rock.
URSULA   But are you sure,
   That Benedick loves Beatrice so entirely?
HERO   So says the prince, and my new trothèd lord.
URSULA   And did they bid you tell her of it, madam?
HERO   They did entreat me to acquaint her of it,   40
   But I persuaded them, if they loved Benedick,
   To wish him wrestle with affection,
   And never to let Beatrice know of it.
URSULA   Why did you so? Doth not the gentleman
   Deserve as full as fortunate a bed,   45
   As ever Beatrice shall couch upon?
HERO   Oh God of love! I know he doth deserve,
   As much as may be yielded to a man:
   But nature never framed a woman's heart
   Of prouder stuff than that of Beatrice: 50
   Disdain and scorn ride sparkling in her eyes,
   Misprising what they look on, and her wit
   Values itself so highly, that to her
   All matter else seems weak: she cannot love,
   Nor take no shape nor project of affection,   55
   She is so self-endeared.
URSULA   Sure I think so,
   And therefore certainly it were not good,
   She knew his love, lest she'll make sport at it.

Hero and Ursula talk about how Beatrice will never admit the true worth of any man, and how she would mock Benedick unmercifully if she knew he loved her. They then praise Benedick's virtues.

---

1 Show how Beatrice mocks all men (in groups of about six)

In lines 59–70 Hero says that Beatrice loves to 'spell backward' every man she meets (i.e. ridicule them by turning their virtues into faults). Choose one man each from: the fair-faced, the black (dark-complexioned), the tall, the low (short), the speaking, the silent.

Each of you draw a caricature picture of your man as Beatrice describes him. Show your group's collection to another group and ask them to match each picture to its appropriate description in the script.

2 Might Hero's criticisms be in earnest? (in pairs)

Some people feel that at least some of Hero's remarks about Beatrice are not comic exaggerations but genuinely felt. Make a list of the faults she finds with her cousin in lines 34–80. Take turns to speak these to each other. Which remarks ring true to you?

As the play will later reveal, Beatrice is not just Hero's cousin but also her most loyal and trusted friend. Why therefore would Hero wish to be so hurtful?

3 'How much an ill word may empoison liking'

Lines 84–6, with their reference to 'honest' (harmless) slanders and 'ill' (slanderous) words poisoning 'liking' (affection), are an ominously ironic reminder for the audience of Don John and Borachio's plot in Act 2 Scene 2 which threatens to ruin Hero's reputation. Turn back to that scene and find the poison image which Hero's words unwittingly echo here.

---

antic grotesque figure
lance ill-headed badly-tipped spear
agate semi-precious stone
vilely cut crudely carved
vane weather vane
gives allows
simpleness simple honesty

purchaseth deserve
carping fault-finding
from all fashions out of step with everyone
press crush beneath a great weight
honest innocent

HERO Why you speak truth, I never yet saw man,
　　　　How wise, how noble, young, how rarely featured,　　　60
　　　　But she would spell him backward: if fair-faced,
　　　　She would swear the gentleman should be her sister:
　　　　If black, why Nature drawing of an antic,
　　　　Made a foul blot: if tall, a lance ill-headed:
　　　　If low, an agate very vilely cut:　　　　　　　　　65
　　　　If speaking, why a vane blown with all winds:
　　　　If silent, why a block moved with none:
　　　　So turns she every man the wrong side out,
　　　　And never gives to truth and virtue, that
　　　　Which simpleness and merit purchaseth.　　　　　70
URSULA Sure, sure, such carping is not commendable.
HERO No, not to be so odd, and from all fashions,
　　　　As Beatrice is, cannot be commendable:
　　　　But who dare tell her so? If I should speak,
　　　　She would mock me into air, oh she would laugh me　75
　　　　Out of myself, press me to death with wit:
　　　　Therefore let Benedick like covered fire,
　　　　Consume away in sighs, waste inwardly:
　　　　It were a better death, than die with mocks,
　　　　Which is as bad as die with tickling.　　　　　80
URSULA Yet tell her of it, hear what she will say.
HERO No rather I will go to Benedick,
　　　　And counsel him to fight against his passion,
　　　　And truly I'll devise some honest slanders,
　　　　To stain my cousin with, one doth not know　　85
　　　　How much an ill word may empoison liking.
URSULA Oh do not do your cousin such a wrong,
　　　　She cannot be so much without true judgement,
　　　　Having so swift and excellent a wit,
　　　　As she is prized to have, as to refuse　　　　90
　　　　So rare a gentleman as Signor Benedick.
HERO He is the only man of Italy,
　　　　Always excepted my dear Claudio.

After more praise of Benedick, Hero and Ursula go inside to choose Hero's head-dress for tomorrow's wedding. Beatrice is amazed by what she has heard and resolves to return Benedick's love.

___

1 Hero's parting couplet (in small groups)

Hero signals her exit with a rhyming couplet (lines 105–6) in which she voices one of the popular sayings of the time. Talk about the way the two pairs of lovers have fallen in love, then decide how much truth there is in what she says. Is falling in love mere chance, or the result of some mysterious power (like the influence of Cupid, the god of love)?

2 A changed Beatrice (in groups of three)

Take it in turns to speak Beatrice's soliloquy (lines 107–16) in different ways (e.g. shocked, deeply moved, comically romantic). Then talk about the following:

a What does Beatrice find more disturbing: Benedick's secret love for her, or the disparaging comments about her 'carping' nature?

b Compare her response with Benedick's (Act 2 Scene 3, lines 181–200). For example, do they both fear being mocked for suddenly falling in love?

c Beatrice speaks for the first time in verse. Does her soliloquy resemble an Elizabethan love sonnet in any way (see p. 188)? Work out the **quatrain** and **couplet** rhyme patterns. Remember that 'I' and '-ly' rhymed in Elizabethan times.

In the early nineteenth century, Beatrice's final soliloquy was often given a comic flavour to parallel Benedick's conversion scene. Most twentieth-century Beatrices have made it a revelation of the serious and tender side of her character. Which interpretation do you prefer and why?

___

Speaking my fancy saying what I think

argument intelligent speech

tomorrow from tomorrow onwards

attires head-dresses or clothes

limed caught, trapped

by haps by chance

No glory . . . such nothing worthwhile is gained by such behaviour

incite thee encourage you

band bond (of marriage)

reportingly just knowing it by what I have heard

URSULA   I pray you be not angry with me, madam,
    Speaking my fancy: Signor Benedick,   95
    For shape, for bearing, argument and valour,
    Goes foremost in report through Italy.
HERO   Indeed he hath an excellent good name.
URSULA   His excellence did earn it, ere he had it:
    When are you married, madam?   100
HERO   Why every day tomorrow: come go in,
    I'll show thee some attires, and have thy counsel,
    Which is the best to furnish me tomorrow.
URSULA   She's limed I warrant you, we have caught her, madam.
HERO   If it prove so, then loving goes by haps,   105
    Some Cupid kills with arrows, some with traps.

Exeunt Hero and Ursula

BEATRICE   What fire is in mine ears? Can this be true?
    Stand I condemned for pride and scorn so much?
    Contempt, farewell, and maiden pride, adieu,
    No glory lives behind the back of such.   110
    And Benedick, love on, I will requite thee,
    Taming my wild heart to thy loving hand:
    If thou dost love, my kindness shall incite thee
    To bind our loves up in a holy band,
    For others say thou dost deserve, and I   115
    Believe it better than reportingly.   *Exit*

Don Pedro plans to return to Arragon as soon as Claudio and Hero are married. The prince, Claudio and Leonato feign amazement at Benedick's lovelorn appearance and behaviour.

1 'Gallants, I am not as I have been' (in groups of four)

Benedick before.   Benedick after.

This is how one artist pictures Benedick's changed appearance. List the differences between these 'before' and 'after' Benedicks. Match each difference to its corresponding line in the scene.

Take a part each and tease Benedick (lines 1–54). In lines 17–19, 'Hang' could mean curse or execute, while 'Draw' could mean pull out or disembowel prior to hanging someone. How do Don Pedro and Claudio play on these words to irritate Benedick?

---

consummate completed
vouchsafe me allow me
soil stain
hangman rascal
humour . . . worm (both were thought to collect in hollow teeth causing toothache – see p. 42)

grief pain
fancy (1) love (2) whim
Dutchman . . . Frenchman . . . (see p. 170)
slops loose, baggy trousers
a brushes he brushes
bode be a sign of

Act 3 Scene 2
Leonato's house

Enter DON PEDRO, CLAUDIO, BENEDICK and LEONATO

DON PEDRO I do but stay till your marriage be consummate, and then
go I toward Arragon.

CLAUDIO I'll bring you thither, my lord, if you'll vouchsafe me.

DON PEDRO Nay that would be as great a soil in the new gloss of your
marriage, as to show a child his new coat and forbid him to wear it: I 5
will only be bold with Benedick for his company, for from the crown
of his head, to the sole of his foot, he is all mirth: he hath twice or
thrice cut Cupid's bow-string, and the little hangman dare not shoot
at him: he hath a heart as sound as a bell, and his tongue is the
clapper, for what his heart thinks, his tongue speaks. 10

BENEDICK Gallants, I am not as I have been.

LEONATO So say I, methinks you are sadder.

CLAUDIO I hope he be in love.

DON PEDRO Hang him, truant, there's no true drop of blood in him to
be truly touched with love: if he be sad, he wants money. 15

BENEDICK I have the tooth-ache.

DON PEDRO Draw it.

BENEDICK Hang it.

CLAUDIO You must hang it first, and draw it afterwards.

DON PEDRO What, sigh for the tooth-ache? 20

LEONATO Where is but a humour or a worm.

BENEDICK Well, everyone cannot master a grief, but he that has it.

CLAUDIO Yet say I, he is in love.

DON PEDRO There is no appearance of fancy in him, unless it be a fancy
that he hath to strange disguises, as to be a Dutchman today, a 25
Frenchman tomorrow, or in the shape of two countries at once, as a
German from the waist downward, all slops, and a Spaniard from
the hip upward, no doublet: unless he have a fancy to this foolery, as
it appears he hath, he is no fool for fancy, as you would have it
appear he is. 30

CLAUDIO If he be not in love with some woman, there is no believing
old signs: a brushes his hat a-mornings, what should that bode?

Benedick's friends continue to joke at his expense. Benedick takes Leonato aside for a private word. Don John interrupts Don Pedro and Claudio's amusement with an ominous-sounding declaration.

1 'She shall be buried with her face upwards'

Don Pedro and Claudio are enjoying embarrassing Benedick. Claudio says that Beatrice 'dies for' Benedick (line 50). 'Dies' was a euphemism for sexual orgasm. So what does Don Pedro mean by his reply?

2 A change of mood (in groups of four)

Someone once commented that whenever Don John appeared he 'felt very much the cool of the evening'. Take parts and read lines 48–69. Make your voices create a sharp change of atmosphere.

Do you think Don Pedro and Claudio's exhilaration at their teasing of Benedick disappears immediately on Don John's entrance or some lines later?

---

stuffed (Elizabethan tennis balls were filled with hair)

civet perfume

paint himself use make-up

For the which . . . him that's what people are saying about him

Nay but his no, that's just his

lute-string a lute was the instrument for love songs

stops frets on the lute

ill conditions bad habits

hobby-horses buffoons

Good den good evening

discover reveal

DON PEDRO Hath any man seen him at the barber's?

CLAUDIO No, but the barber's man hath been seen with him, and the old ornament of his cheek hath already stuffed tennis balls. 35

LEONATO Indeed he looks younger than he did, by the loss of a beard.

DON PEDRO Nay, a rubs himself with civet, can you smell him out by that?

CLAUDIO That's as much as to say, the sweet youth's in love.

DON PEDRO The greatest note of it is his melancholy. 40

CLAUDIO And when was he wont to wash his face?

DON PEDRO Yea, or to paint himself? For the which I hear what they say of him.

CLAUDIO Nay but his jesting spirit, which is now crept into a lute-string, and now governed by stops. 45

DON PEDRO Indeed that tells a heavy tale for him: conclude, conclude, he is in love.

CLAUDIO Nay but I know who loves him.

DON PEDRO That would I know too, I warrant one that knows him not.

CLAUDIO Yes, and his ill conditions, and in despite of all, dies for him. 50

DON PEDRO She shall be buried with her face upwards.

BENEDICK Yet is this no charm for the tooth-ache: old signor, walk aside with me, I have studied eight or nine wise words to speak to you, which these hobby-horses must not hear.

[Exeunt Benedick and Leonato]

DON PEDRO For my life, to break with him about Beatrice. 55

CLAUDIO 'Tis even so: Hero and Margaret have by this played their parts with Beatrice, and then the two bears will not bite one another when they meet.

Enter DON JOHN *the Bastard*

DON JOHN My lord and brother, God save you.

DON PEDRO Good den, brother. 60

DON JOHN If your leisure served, I would speak with you.

DON PEDRO In private?

DON JOHN If it please you, yet Count Claudio may hear, for what I would speak of, concerns him.

DON PEDRO What's the matter? 65

DON JOHN Means your lordship to be married tomorrow?

DON PEDRO You know he does.

DON JOHN I know not that, when he knows what I know.

CLAUDIO If there be any impediment, I pray you discover it.

Don John claims that he has proof of Hero's infidelity. He invites Claudio and Don Pedro to witness Hero's unfaithful behaviour. They vow to shame her in public if she is proved unchaste.

---

1 Hear the male anger (in groups of three)

Take a part each and sit facing each other. Read aloud lines 75–100 looking into each other's eyes. How would you describe the manner in which Don John speaks to the other two?

Read aloud lines 91–100. Sound angry and vengeful. Spit out the consonants (especially the 'd's, 't's and 's's). What animal does Don John remind you of as he speaks his final words?

These three men are quickly united in their anger at Hero's presumed 'infidelity'. How do the patterns of their sentences from line 88 onwards emphasise this union of male hostility?

2 Why trust Don John? (in small groups)

The prince's brother has already provoked a war and attempted to spoil Claudio's betrothal to Hero. Yet both Claudio and Don Pedro again seem all too ready to believe him. What key words does Don John use in lines 78–85 to prick the pride of these powerful men? (It may help your understanding to read pp. 165, 168 and 178.)

3 'If you dare not trust that you see'

In line 88 Don John seems to be saying 'If you are not prepared to trust the evidence of your own eyes, then you can never say that you know anything'. We know that Claudio and Don Pedro should not believe what they are about to 'see' at Hero's bedroom window. Which other characters have already been deceived by what they have 'noted' with their own eyes?

---

aim better at me   judge me better
holp to effect   helped to bring about
suit ill-spent   effort wasted
ill-bestowed   misused
circumstances shortened   to put it briefly

paint out   depict in full
warrant   proof
bear it coldly   control your anger
issue   outcome
untowardly   unfavourably
mischief   misfortune

DON JOHN You may think I love you not, let that appear hereafter, and   70
  aim better at me by that I now will manifest, for my brother (I think
  he holds you well, and in dearness of heart) hath holp to effect your
  ensuing marriage: surely suit ill-spent, and labour ill-bestowed.

DON PEDRO Why what's the matter?

DON JOHN I came hither to tell you, and circumstances shortened (for   75
  she has been too long a-talking of), the lady is disloyal.

CLAUDIO Who Hero?

DON JOHN Even she, Leonato's Hero, your Hero, every man's Hero.

CLAUDIO Disloyal?

DON JOHN The word is too good to paint out her wickedness, I could   80
  say she were worse, think you of a worse title, and I will fit her to it:
  wonder not till further warrant: go but with me tonight, you shall see
  her chamber window entered, even the night before her wedding
  day: if you love her, then tomorrow wed her: but it would better fit
  your honour to change your mind.   85

CLAUDIO May this be so?

DON PEDRO I will not think it.

DON JOHN If you dare not trust that you see, confess not that you know:
  if you will follow me, I will show you enough: and when you have
  seen more, and heard more, proceed accordingly.   90

CLAUDIO If I see anything tonight, why I should not marry her tomorrow in the congregation, where I should wed, there will I shame her.

DON PEDRO And as I wooed for thee to obtain her, I will join with thee,
  to disgrace her.

DON JOHN I will disparage her no farther, till you are my witnesses: bear 95
  it coldly but till midnight, and let the issue show itself.

DON PEDRO Oh day untowardly turned!

CLAUDIO Oh mischief strangely thwarting!

DON JOHN Oh plague right well prevented! So will you say, when you
  have seen the sequel.   100

                                                              Exeunt

Dogberry, the Master Constable, and Verges, his deputy, assemble the Town Watch and set about appointing a constable to oversee the activities of the Watchmen.

---

1 Enter the clowns (in groups of five)

No sooner has Don John begun to weave his evil plot, than Shakespeare introduces the simple, ordinary men whose dramatic function it will be to bring the villain and his henchmen to justice.

The Watch were the policemen of Shakespeare's day, their incompetence a standing joke with Elizabethan playwrights. Shakespeare's Watchmen are very English, with English names and attitudes, and they are spectacularly inept.

Will Kemp, the resident comedian in Shakespeare's company, was probably the first to play the part of Dogberry. Kemp relied for laughs on clowning, grimaces and ad lib remarks.

To get a first impression of how these men think and behave, share out the parts of Dogberry, Verges, Seacoal, Watchman 1 and Watchman 2 and read through lines 1–77.

2 Dogberry, a comic mangler of words (in small groups)

Dogberry attempts to give his words an imposing ring, but the results are often baffling. Find one or two sentences or phrases that sound impressive but are really absolute nonsense.

Dogberry's particular talent is for **malapropisms** (the mistaken use of words – see p. 185). For example, he says 'desartless' (line 8) when he means 'deserving'. Use the glosses below to find other malapropisms and then devise your own version of lines 1–22 entitled 'Dogberry Corrected', in which Dogberry speaks and the others in the group find ways of intervening to correct his mistakes.

---

it were pity but   it would be a pity if
salvation   he means 'damnation'
allegiance   he means 'disloyalty'
give them their charge   explain their duties
Seacoal . . . name   because coal is a blessing from God

well-favoured   good-looking
nature   he means 'nurture'
favour   appearance
senseless   he means 'sensible'
comprehend   he means 'apprehend'
vagrom   he means 'vagrant'
stand   stop

Act 3 Scene 3
Near Leonato's house

Enter DOGBERRY and his partner VERGES with SEACOAL,
WATCHMAN 1, WATCHMAN 2 and the rest of the Watch

DOGBERRY Are you good men and true?

VERGES Yea, or else it were pity but they should suffer salvation body
and soul.

DOGBERRY Nay, that were a punishment too good for them, if they
should have any allegiance in them, being chosen for the prince's   5
watch.

VERGES Well, give them their charge, neighbour Dogberry.

DOGBERRY First, who think you the most desartless man to be
constable?

WATCHMAN 1 Hugh Oatcake, sir, or George Seacoal, for they can   10
write and read.

DOGBERRY Come hither, neighbour Seacoal, God hath blessed you
with a good name: to be a well-favoured man, is the gift of Fortune,
but to write and read, comes by nature.

SEACOAL Both which, master constable –   15

DOGBERRY You have: I knew it would be your answer: well, for your
favour, sir, why give God thanks, and make no boast of it, and for
your writing and reading, let that appear when there is no need of
such vanity: you are thought here to be the most senseless and fit
man for the constable of the watch: therefore bear you the lantern: 20
this is your charge, you shall comprehend all vagrom men, you are
to bid any man stand, in the prince's name.

Dogberry outlines the duties required of the Watch in maintaining law and order. He advises them to avoid getting involved with criminals and troublemakers, and tells them that it's far better to go to sleep!

1 'Read all about it!' (in small groups)

List all the crimes in lines 21–77 which might go undetected due to the laziness and timidity of the Watch. Add to your list any other 'crime' which you know has taken place that night.

Two of you are newspaper-sellers shouting out the news headlines telling of last night's crimes. The rest are the Watchmen, commenting unofficially on what they were doing when the crimes were committed.

2 The forces of law and order

The 1988 Royal Shakespeare Company production set the play in the 1950s on a sunlit terrace with sunbathers, swimming pools and glasses of champagne. This picture shows the Watch. Identify the characters.

How if a will not stand? What if he will not stop?
bidden ordered to
tolerable he means 'intolerable'
belongs to is the proper thing for
ancient experienced
bills pikes or halberds, weapons

true man honest man
meddle or make concern yourselves
the more . . . honesty the better it is for your reputation
hang a dog animals could be charged with offences in the sixteenth century

SEACOAL How if a will not stand?

DOGBERRY Why then take no note of him, but let him go, and presently
call the rest of the watch together, and thank God you are rid of a   25
knave.

VERGES If he will not stand when he is bidden, he is none of the prince's
subjects.

DOGBERRY True, and they arc to meddle with none but the prince's
subjects: you shall also make no noise in the streets: for, for the   30
watch to babble and to talk, is most tolerable and not to be endured.

WATCHMAN 2 We will rather sleep than talk, we know what belongs to
a watch.

DOGBERRY Why you speak like an ancient and most quiet watchman,
for I cannot see how sleeping should offend: only have a care that   35
your bills be not stolen: well, you are to call at all the alehouses, and
bid those that are drunk get them to bed.

SEACOAL How if they will not?

DOGBERRY Why then let them alone till they are sober: if they make you
not then the better answer, you may say, they are not the men you   40
took them for.

SEACOAL Well, sir.

DOGBERRY If you meet a thief, you may suspect him, by virtue of your
office, to be no true man: and for such kind of men, the less you
meddle or make with them, why the more is for your honesty.   45

SEACOAL If we know him to be a thief, shall we not lay hands on him?

DOGBERRY Truly by your office you may, but I think they that touch
pitch will be defiled: the most peaceable way for you, if you do take a
thief, is, to let him show himself what he is, and steal out of your
company.   50

VERGES You have been always called a merciful man, partner.

DOGBERRY Truly I would not hang a dog by my will, much more a man
who hath any honesty in him.

After giving more advice, Dogberry and Verges leave. As the Watch make themselves comfortable on the church bench, Borachio and Conrade enter, unaware that they are being observed.

1 Stage the eavesdropping and capture

This is the new reconstructed Globe Theatre (see pp. 190–1), where it undoubtedly does sometimes 'drizzle rain' (lines 86–7). Notice the two pillars supporting the 'penthouse' (overhanging roof) and the actors' entrance doors left and right. The central section can also be opened to reveal a small 'inner room'. Draw a plan with notes detailing props, movements and so on, indicating how you would use this stage to present the moment when the plot to ruin Hero is overheard (lines 70–147).

---

present   he means 'represent'
by'r Lady   by Our Lady (an oath)
a cannot   he cannot
Five . . . on't   I bet you five shillings to one
and there . . . chances   if anything important happens

keep . . . own   be discreet
coil   hustle and bustle
vigitant   he means 'vigilant'
Mass   by the Holy Mass (an oath)
scab   also means villain
I will owe . . . for that   I'll get you back for that

VERGES If you hear a child cry in the night, you must call to the nurse
and bid her still it. 55

WATCHMAN 2 How if the nurse be asleep and will not hear us?

DOGBERRY Why then depart in peace, and let the child wake her with
crying, for the ewe that will not hear her lamb when it baas, will
never answer a calf when he bleats.

VERGES 'Tis very true. 60

DOGBERRY This is the end of the charge: you, constable, are to present
the prince's own person, if you meet the prince in the night, you may
stay him.

VERGES Nay by'r Lady that I think a cannot.

DOGBERRY Five shillings to one on't with any man that knows the 65
statutes, he may stay him: marry, not without the prince be willing,
for indeed the watch ought to offend no man, and it is an offence to
stay a man against his will.

VERGES By'r Lady I think it be so.

DOGBERRY Ha, ah ha! Well, masters, good night: and there be any 70
matter of weight chances, call up me: keep your fellows' counsels,
and your own, and good night: come, neighbour.

SEACOAL Well masters, we hear our charge, let us go sit here upon the
church bench till two, and then all to bed.

DOGBERRY One word more, honest neighbours, I pray you watch about 75
Signor Leonato's door, for the wedding being there tomorrow,
there is a great coil tonight: adieu, be vigitant I beseech you.

Exeunt [*Dogberry and Verges*]

Enter BORACHIO *and* CONRADE

BORACHIO What, Conrade?

SEACOAL Peace, stir not.

BORACHIO Conrade, I say. 80

CONRADE Here, man, I am at thy elbow.

BORACHIO Mass and my elbow itched, I thought there would a scab
follow.

CONRADE I will owe thee an answer for that, and now forward with thy
tale. 85

BORACHIO Stand thee close then under this penthouse, for it drizzles
rain, and I will, like a true drunkard, utter all to thee.

The drunken Borachio starts to tell Conrade about the villainous deed he has done that very night. He then digresses to talk about the influence of fashion on wealthy young gentlemen. The Watch listen, bemused.

---

1 Fashion and appearance, reality and truth (in pairs)

Nearly everyone in the play finds it hard to distinguish appearance from reality. The drunken Borachio has just seen how a rich villain (Don John) can simply buy the kind of 'truth' he wants. Now he ponders on the behaviour of the young aristocrats of the day, giddily seeking the latest fashions.

Borachio's words puzzle Conrade. Read lines 89–117 (Conrade can also speak as the Watchman). Express Borachio's drunkenness and Conrade's growing exasperation.

a **'What a deformed thief this fashion is'** The remark is said twice and echoed a third time in lines 101–7, so the audience are meant to 'note' it. Elizabethan fashions, with their padding and strange shapes (see pp. 170–3), certainly 'de-formed' the human figure. But what other meanings might this remark have? For example, what has fashion or costume 'stolen' from Hero and Benedick?

b **'I know that Deformed'** The Watchman (lines 103–4) is completely foxed. What does *he* think Borachio is talking about?

c **'How giddily [fashion] turns about all the hot-bloods'** Late sixteenth-century Elizabethan fashions were elaborate, fantastic and changed with bewildering speed. Borachio (lines 109–13) gives three examples of the kind of costumes that these young 'hot-bloods' copied: those of Pharaoh's soldiers, Bel's priests and Hercules. Where does Borachio say each picture may be found?

Find the remark by Conrade which suggests that he, like Borachio, believed that the Elizabethans changed their taste in fashion too easily.

---

stand close   keep quiet
be so rich   pay so much
make   ask
unconfirmed   inexperienced, naive
nothing to a man   no indication of what the man is really like
Tush   nonsense

a   he (as in 'a has', 'a turns')
vane   weathervane (What might this have to do with fashions?)
reechy   dirty, filthy
god Bel   a heathen god
cod-piece   a man's genital pouch
massy   massive

SEACOAL Some treason, masters, yet stand close.

BORACHIO Therefore know, I have earned of Don John a thousand
ducats. 90

CONRADE Is it possible that any villainy should be so dear?

BORACHIO Thou shouldst rather ask if it were possible any villainy
should be so rich. For when rich villains have need of poor ones,
poor ones may make what price they will.

CONRADE I wonder at it. 95

BORACHIO That shows thou art unconfirmed: thou knowest that the
fashion of a doublet, or a hat, or a cloak, is nothing to a man.

CONRADE Yes, it is apparel.

BORACHIO I mean the fashion.

CONRADE Yes, the fashion is the fashion. 100

BORACHIO Tush, I may as well say the fool's the fool, but seest thou not
what a deformed thief this fashion is?

WATCHMAN 1 I know that Deformed, a has been a vile thief, this seven
year, a goes up and down like a gentleman: I remember his name.

BORACHIO Didst thou not hear somebody? 105

CONRADE No, 'twas the vane on the house.

BORACHIO Seest thou not, I say, what a deformed thief this fashion is,
how giddily a turns about all the hot-bloods, between fourteen and
five and thirty, sometimes fashioning them like Pharaoh's soldiers in
the reechy painting, sometime like god Bel's priests in the old 110
church window, sometime like the shaven Hercules in the smirched
worm-eaten tapestry, where his cod-piece seems as massy as his
club?

CONRADE All this I see, and I see that the fashion wears out more
apparel than the man: but art not thou thyself giddy with the fashion 115
too, that thou hast shifted out of thy tale into telling me of the
fashion?

Borachio tells Conrade the details of how he deceived Don Pedro and Claudio. The Watch arrest the two villains and lead them away.

1 Borachio's story (in groups of about six)

Borachio is drunk and, as he himself admits, tells his tale 'vilely'. Read lines 118–33 and rehearse a properly ordered version of his story (it could begin 'I should first tell thee how . . .'). One narrates while the others act out the events, perhaps in mime or using improvised dialogue.

2 A comic or dramatic arrest? (in groups of about six)

In one production a huge, hulking watchman accidentally felled two of his companions before beating Borachio and Conrade into submission.

Rehearse lines 130 (from 'away went Claudio . . .') to the end of the scene. Make sure all your moves are absolutely safe! One Elizabethan actor was killed as he rehearsed a fight scene, when an opponent's sword pierced through his eye and entered his brain. So find some suitably harmless 'weapons'.

If you take time to memorise your lines it will be much more effective. Try it in two ways:

- Play it for comedy. The Watch are frightened and incompetent, while Borachio and Conrade are drunk and incapable.
- But what if the villains had resisted? Elizabethan gentlemen carried swords and often used them. This time the Watch (despite Dogberry's advice) should be brave and determined, and the villains prepared to fight and kill.

Show both versions to the rest of the class and decide which is the more appropriate for this scene.

---

possessed convinced, evilly influenced
o'er night the night before
right honourable, worthy
recovered/lechery he means 'discovered' and 'treachery'
commonwealth state, country

lock a long curl of hair or lovelock (see pp. 170–1)
obey Seacoal means 'order'
commodity goods for sale
bills (1) weapons (2) credit notes
in question highly sought after

BORACHIO Not so neither, but know that I have tonight wooed Margaret, the Lady Hero's gentlewoman, by the name of Hero: she leans me out at her mistress' chamber window, bids me a thousand 120 times good night: I tell this tale vilely, I should first tell thee how the prince, Claudio and my master planted, and placed, and possessed, by my master Don John, saw afar off in the orchard this amiable encounter.

CONRADE And thought they Margaret was Hero? 125

BORACHIO Two of them did, the prince and Claudio, but the devil my master knew she was Margaret, and partly by his oaths, which first possessed them, partly by the dark night which did deceive them, but chiefly, by my villainy, which did confirm any slander that Don John had made – away went Claudio enraged, swore he would meet 130 her as he was appointed next morning at the temple, and there, before the whole congregation shame her, with what he saw o'er night, and send her home again without a husband.

SEACOAL We charge you in the prince's name, stand.

WATCHMAN 2 Call up the right master constable, we have here 135 recovered the most dangerous piece of lechery, that ever was known in the commonwealth.

WATCHMAN 1 And one Deformed is one of them, I know him, a wears a lock.

CONRADE Masters, masters. 140

WATCHMAN 1 You'll be made bring Deformed forth I warrant you.

SEACOAL Masters, never speak, we charge you, let us obey you to go with us.

BORACHIO We are like to prove a goodly commodity, being taken up of these men's bills. 145

CONRADE A commodity in question I warrant you: come, we'll obey you.

Exeunt

It is the morning of the wedding and Hero, with Margaret to help her, prepares herself. At first the talk is of fashion, but Margaret turns the conversation to sex.

---

1 The height of fashion

Portrait of Lady Elizabeth Southwell, a maid of honour to Queen Elizabeth (1599).

The rich fabrics of Lady Southwell's gown (right) are woven with gold and silver thread ('cloth o'gold'), on which are sewn jewels and pearls. In places there are 'cuts' in the material to show off the contrasting fabrics beneath.

Note the wired neck ruff or 'rebato', the 'tire' (wired head-dress decorated with jewels and false curls), the wide 'down sleeves' and the loose, hanging 'side sleeves'.

The down sleeves and the V-shaped stomacher are heavily padded. The huge skirt is 'round underborne' (stiffened with material on the inside) and shaped with padding and wire supports.

Read lines 1–18 and decide how closely the Duchess of Milan's and Hero's gowns match this portrait. In what way do they remind you of Borachio's observation in the previous scene (line 107) that fashion is 'a deformed thief'?

By my troth's   in truth it is
within   (inside the neck ruff)
a thought   a shade
exceeds   excels
night-gown   dressing gown
quaint   elegant, dainty
on't   of it

and bad thinking . . . speaking   so long as bad thoughts do not twist the meaning of good words
and it be   if it be
light   can also mean 'immoral'
else   otherwise

Act 3 Scene 4
Hero's dressing room

Enter HERO and MARGARET and URSULA

HERO Good Ursula, wake my cousin Beatrice, and desire her to rise.

URSULA I will, lady.

HERO And bid her come hither.

URSULA Well.   [*Exit*]

MARGARET Troth I think your other rebato were better.   5

HERO No pray thee, good Meg, I'll wear this.

MARGARET By my troth's not so good, and I warrant your cousin will say so.

HERO My cousin's a fool, and thou art another, I'll wear none but this.

MARGARET I like the new tire within excellently, if the hair were a   10
thought browner: and your gown's a most rare fashion i'faith. I saw
the Duchess of Milan's gown that they praise so.

HERO Oh, that exceeds they say.

MARGARET By my troth's but a night-gown in respect of yours, cloth
o'gold and cuts, and laced with silver, set with pearls, down sleeves,   15
side sleeves, and skirts, round underborne with a bluish tinsel – but
for a fine quaint graceful and excellent fashion, yours is worth ten
on't.

HERO God give me joy to wear it, for my heart is exceeding heavy.

MARGARET 'Twill be heavier soon by the weight of a man.   20

HERO Fie upon thee, art not ashamed?

MARGARET Of what, lady? Of speaking honourably? Is not marriage
honourable in a beggar? Is not your lord honourable without marriage? I think you would have me say, saving your reverence, a
husband: and bad thinking do not wrest true speaking, I'll offend   25
nobody: is there any harm in the heavier for a husband? None I think,
and it be the right husband, and the right wife, otherwise 'tis light
and not heavy: ask my Lady Beatrice else, here she comes.

Beatrice enters suffering from a heavy cold. Margaret hints very pointedly that Beatrice is out of sorts because of her love for Benedick.

1 Tease Beatrice (in groups of about six)

This scene echoes the friends' mockery of Benedick in Act 3 Scene 2. Just as love has given Benedick toothache, it has now given Beatrice a cold. Three of you read lines 29–70. The others echo Margaret's words to Beatrice in a teasing manner.

2 Quick-witted women (in groups of three)

Margaret takes the lead in teasing Beatrice, hoping perhaps to match Beatrice's wit while she is temporarily off form. Take parts and rehearse your comic version of lines 33–70. Use the following explanations of the wordplay to help you:

Light o'Love (meaning 'joy of love') was a popular dance song of the day (lines 33–7). Margaret claims to want Beatrice to sing it because it needs no bass or male accompaniment ('goes without a burden'). This of course continues the pun on 'lightness', because 'light o'love' could also mean 'loose woman'. Beatrice takes up the hint with her use of 'heels' and 'barns'. Kicking up your heels also suggested sexual promiscuity, while 'barns' puns on 'bairns' (children). What other sexual innuendoes can you find in the script opposite?

Carduus benedictus is the Latin name for Holy Thistle (line 60), a popular and fashionable remedy for many complaints, especially 'perilous diseases of the heart'. In lines 52–61, one Beatrice put a cloth over her head as she said, 'by my troth I am sick', popped her head out in surprise at Margaret's joke about getting some 'distilled *Carduus benedictus*' for her cold, then covered her head again when Margaret said, 'you may think perchance that I think you are in love' (lines 60–1).

Clap's into let us strike up	**star** Pole (or fixed) Star
heigh ho a sigh ('heigh'), also a cry used in hawking and riding	**trow** I wonder
H (i.e. 'ache' which was sometimes pronounced 'aitch')	**stuffed** blocked nose, or pregnant
	apprehension wit
and . . . Turk if you have changed your beliefs (about love)	**cap** i.e. your fool's cap
	qualm sudden sickness

Enter BEATRICE

HERO Good morrow, coz.

BEATRICE Good morrow, sweet Hero.   30

HERO Why how now? Do you speak in the sick tune?

BEATRICE I am out of all other tune, methinks.

MARGARET Clap's into *Light o'Love*: that goes without a burden: do you
  sing it and I'll dance it.

BEATRICE Ye light o'love with your heels, then if your husband have   35
  stables enough, you'll see he shall lack no barns.

MARGARET Oh illegitimate construction! I scorn that with my heels.

BEATRICE 'Tis almost five o'clock, cousin, 'tis time you were ready: by
  my troth I am exceeding ill, heigh ho.

MARGARET For a hawk, a horse, or a husband?   40

BEATRICE For the letter that begins them all, H.

MARGARET Well, and you be not turned Turk, there's no more sailing
  by the star.

BEATRICE What means the fool, trow?

MARGARET Nothing I, but God send everyone their heart's desire.   45

HERO These gloves the count sent me, they are an excellent perfume.

BEATRICE I am stuffed, cousin, I cannot smell.

MARGARET A maid and stuffed! There's goodly catching of cold.

BEATRICE Oh God help me, God help me, how long have you professed apprehension?   50

MARGARET Ever since you left it: doth not my wit become me rarely?

BEATRICE It is not seen enough, you should wear it in your cap: by my
  troth I am sick.

MARGARET Get you some of this distilled *Carduus benedictus*, and lay it
  to your heart, it is the only thing for a qualm.   55

HERO There thou prick'st her with a thistle.

BEATRICE *Benedictus*, why *benedictus*? You have some moral in this
  benedictus.

Margaret chatters teasingly to Beatrice about love and Benedick. Ursula
returns with the news that the men have arrived to take Hero to the church.

1 Thoughts before the wedding

List the different moods and attitudes to marriage expressed by
Beatrice, Hero and Margaret in this scene. Despite the gentle teasing,
there is a sense of sadness and poignancy. Write a paragraph about
what the facial expressions of each of these women tell you of their
unspoken thoughts.

2 How could Margaret compromise Hero? (in groups of three)

Margaret, a gentlewoman, is not a lowly servant, but neither is she
the social equal of Hero or Beatrice. Decide whether she behaves in
this scene like a woman foolish enough to be duped by Borachio into
posing as Hero at her mistress's bedroom window.

Take a part each and read through the whole scene. Then take it
in turns to read Margaret's lines 59–68. Try pausing for breath only
when you meet a colon or full stop. Which four words or phrases best
sum up Margaret's personality?

Moral / moral meaning   hidden
 meaning
by my troth   on my honour
by'r Lady   by Our Lady (a mild oath)
list   (1) please (2) wish
such another   i.e. another one who
 would never fall in love

eats . . . grudging   accepts his
 destiny (of getting married) without
 complaint
Not a false gallop   I speak the truth (a
 false gallop, or canter, is not a natural
 pace for a horse)
gallants   fine gentlemen

MARGARET Moral? No by my troth, I have no moral meaning, I meant
plain Holy Thistle, you may think perchance that I think you are in   60
love, nay by'r Lady I am not such a fool to think what I list, nor I list
not to think what I can, nor indeed I cannot think, if I would think
my heart out of thinking, that you are in love, or that you will be in
love, or that you can be in love: yet Benedick was such another, and
now is he become a man, he swore he would never marry, and yet   65
now in despite of his heart he eats his meat without grudging, and
how you may be converted I know not, but methinks you look with
your eyes as other women do.
BEATRICE What pace is this that thy tongue keeps?
MARGARET Not a false gallop.   70

Enter URSULA

URSULA Madam, withdraw, the prince, the count, Signor Benedick,
Don John, and all the gallants of the town are come to fetch you to
church.
HERO Help to dress me, good coz, good Meg, good Ursula.

[Exeunt]

Leonato is busy with the last-minute preparations for the wedding. Dogberry and Verges come to inform him of the arrest of Borachio and Conrade, but their ramblings exasperate the impatient Leonato.

---

1 Don't interrupt me now (in groups of three)

Ironically, in his anxiety to get to his daughter's wedding, Leonato is unaware of the importance of this interview. For their part, Dogberry and Verges are equally unaware of how vital their news is.

Take a part each (ignore lines 42–4) and read the scene through. Dogberry and Verges should be very respectful, but rambling and 'tedious'. Leonato should be flustered, irritable and anxious to leave. Can you decide where Dogberry talks to Leonato and where he talks to Verges?

2 Another batch of words bites the dust (in small groups)

It is not easy to insult Dogberry. Leonato tells him that he is 'tedious' (line 14). Dogberry assumes 'tedious' means 'rich' and very charitably says that if he *were* rich he would gladly give all his 'tediousness' to Leonato! Here are other words Dogberry misuses and mangles in this scene:

decerns (line 3)	*comprehended* (line 35)
blunt (line 9)	*aspitious* (line 36)
odorous (line 13)	*suffigance* (line 40)
exclamation ('loud complaint' – line 20)	*examination* (line 46)

Take turns to speak the sentences where Dogberry uses these words and decide what he means to say in each case. Compare your ideas with another group's.

Headborough Deputy Constable	**palabras** means 'words' (in Spanish!)
Marry indeed	**poor duke's officers** he means the
nearly closely	duke's poor officers
Brief Be brief	**of your worship** on your worship
Goodman title for a man below the	**exclamation on** loud complaint about
rank of gentleman	**fain know** appreciate knowing

Act 3 Scene 5
The hall of Leonato's house

Enter LEONATO and DOGBERRY the Constable and VERGES the
Headborough

LEONATO What would you with me, honest neighbour?

DOGBERRY Marry, sir, I would have some confidence with you, that
   decerns you nearly.

LEONATO Brief I pray you, for you see it is a busy time with me.

DOGBERRY Marry this it is, sir.   5

VERGES Yes in truth it is, sir.

LEONATO What is it, my good friends?

DOGBERRY Goodman Verges, sir, speaks a little off the matter, an old
   man, sir, and his wits are not so blunt, as God help I would desire
   they were, but in faith honest, as the skin between his brows.   10

VERGES Yes I thank God, I am honest as any man living, that is an old
   man, and no honester than I.

DOGBERRY Comparisons are odorous, palabras, neighbour Verges.

LEONATO Neighbours, you are tedious.

DOGBERRY It pleases your worship to say so, but we are the poor duke's 15
   officers, but truly for mine own part, if I were as tedious as a king, I
   could find in my heart to bestow it all of your worship.

LEONATO All thy tediousness on me, ah?

DOGBERRY Yea, and 'twere a thousand pound more than 'tis, for I hear
   as good exclamation on your worship as of any man in the city, and   20
   though I be but a poor man, I am glad to hear it.

VERGES And so am I.

LEONATO I would fain know what you have to say.

Leonato cannot wait for Dogberry to get to the point. He instructs Dogberry to conduct the trial, not realising the significance for himself and his daughter of the crime that has been uncovered.

1 Impressive stupidity (in groups of three)

Dogberry sees himself as far superior to his partner Verges. Take the parts of Dogberry, Verges and Leonato and rehearse lines 24–34. Show Dogberry's patronising self-importance and Leonato's amused sarcasm.

If Dogberry has a high opinion of his own intelligence, where do you think he points when he says 'here's that shall drive some of them to a noncome' (lines 49–50)?

Is this how you imagined these three men might look? Find the line in this scene which suggests that Dogberry is a much larger man than Verges.

excepting   Verges means 'respecting'
ha' ta'en   have arrested
arrant   out-and-out
world   wonder
and two . . . horse   if two men ride on one horse (i.e. there can only be one leader)

stay for you   wait for you
Francis Seacoal   Does he mean George Seacoal of Act 3 Scene 3?
noncome   out of their wits
only   just

VERGES Marry, sir, our watch tonight, excepting your worship's presence, ha' ta'en a couple of as arrant knaves as any in Messina. 25

DOGBERRY A good old man, sir, he will be talking as they say, when the age is in, the wit is out, God help us, it is a world to see: well said i'faith, neighbour Verges, well, God's a good man, and two men ride of a horse, one must ride behind, an honest soul i'faith, sir, by my troth he is, as ever broke bread, but God is to be worshipped, all 30
men are not alike, alas, good neighbour.

LEONATO Indeed, neighbour, he comes too short of you.

DOGBERRY Gifts that God gives.

LEONATO I must leave you.

DOGBERRY One word, sir, our watch, sir, have indeed comprehended 35
two aspitious persons, and we would have them this morning examined before your worship.

LEONATO Take their examination yourself, and bring it me, I am now in great haste, as it may appear unto you.

DOGBERRY It shall be suffigance. 40

[*Enter* MESSENGER]

LEONATO Drink some wine ere you go: fare you well.

MESSENGER My lord, they stay for you, to give your daughter to her husband.

LEONATO I'll wait upon them, I am ready.

Exit [Leonato with Messenger]

DOGBERRY Go, good partner, go get you to Francis Seacoal, bid him 45
bring his pen and ink-horn to the gaol: we are now to examination these men.

VERGES And we must do it wisely.

DOGBERRY We will spare for no wit I warrant you: here's that shall drive some of them to a noncome, only get the learned writer to set down 50
our excommunication, and meet me at the gaol.

Exeunt

Looking back at Act 3
Activities for groups or individuals

1 A profoundly shaken Beatrice overhears Margaret and Hero

Act out Beatrice's dream on the night before Hero's wedding. Who might visit her in her dream and what might they say? Think about how her subconscious mind might explore Hero's 'criticism' of her (Act 3 Scene 1, lines 47–56), as well as her feelings for Benedick.

2 Dark and light (in groups of six or more)

As the play moves towards its crisis, Shakespeare alternates the two main plots (Beatrice–Benedick and Hero–Claudio) and thus shifts the mood of the play continually from comedy to potential tragedy.

Present a five-minute version of Act 3. Speed up the comic moments and make the threatening or serious moments seem slow and intense.

3 Compare Claudio and Benedick

The two friends, Claudio and Benedick, are in love with the two main female characters. Write notes on Benedick's love story, then do the same for Claudio.

Compare the stories and the behaviour of the two men. Which man feels love more deeply and sincerely? Which do you find the more attractive and likeable?

4 The Watch

Jot down as many reasons as you can for the Watch being in the play (p. 180 may help you). Dogberry and his men did not feature at all in Acts 1 and 2. Write a paragraph suggesting why they now suddenly play such a prominent part in events.

5 Opinion polls (in small groups)

Carry out a survey in your group of the five most likeable characters in the play and the five most disliked. Draw up your lists in order of rank. Ask those you interview to give reasons for their choices. Present your findings as a display of some kind.

6 How different are men and women? (in small groups)

a Extend Act 3 Scene 2. Improvise a two-minute exchange between Claudio and Don Pedro which takes place after Don John has left. Show Claudio's anger, resentment and wounded pride. Show as clearly as you can what you think these men are most worried about.

b Present a two-minute version of Act 3 Scene 4. Show the women's optimism, teasing and mutual concern as they prepare for Hero's wedding. Don't forget there are also moments of foreboding. What are the women's main concerns?

c After watching the other groups' presentations of 'men together' and 'women together', list the differences you have noticed.

The guests assemble for the wedding of Hero and Claudio. As Friar Francis begins the marriage ceremony, Claudio refuses to accept Hero as his bride and hands her back to Leonato.

1 A very public rejection (in large groups)

In Shakespeare's time, marriages among the aristocracy were arranged as family bargains, and an unchaste bride was a worthless thing (see p. 168). Several times, with bitter irony, Claudio calls Hero a 'maid'.

Rehearse the dramatic opening moments of this wedding scene (lines 1–31). Create a happy and holy atmosphere as the wedding guests assemble, then a contrast as Claudio begins his denunciation of Hero. Think about Leonato's behaviour as father of the bride and the possible reasons for Benedick's strange interruption. Just how does Claudio return Hero to her father?

2 ''Tis pity she's a whore' (in groups of about six)

One person speaks Claudio's opening accusations of Hero (lines 25–55). The others express their reactions in the following ways:

Disbelief Claudio speaks his lines face to face with Hero. The rest act as family and friends. Echo the words and phrases you find unbelievable. At the end, ask Hero to say what she is thinking.

Support Repeat the exercise, but now the group members are, like Don Pedro, supporters of Claudio and echo words that emphasise Claudio's anger and disgust. At the end, ask Hero how she feels.

3 'This rotten orange'

Why should Claudio choose the image of an orange to describe Hero? Write it down and, as you read on, write other words and phrases around it from lines 1–104 which are connected in some way to the image of a rotten orange.

---

plain form simpler version
inward secret
Interjections interruptions
Stand thee by stand to one side
unconstrainèd unforced
counterpoise be of equal weight to
render her give her back

learn me teach me
semblance appearance
maid innocent virgin
what : . . truth what appearance of
  authority and truth
withal with

Act 4 Scene 1
A church

Enter DON PEDRO, DON JOHN, LEONATO, FRIAR FRANCIS, CLAUDIO, BENEDICK, HERO and BEATRICE; Wedding Guests

LEONATO Come, Friar Francis, be brief, only to the plain form of
marriage, and you shall recount their particular duties afterwards.

FRIAR FRANCIS You come hither, my lord, to marry this lady?

CLAUDIO No.

LEONATO To be married to her: friar, you come to marry her. 5

FRIAR FRANCIS Lady, you come hither to be married to this count?

HERO I do.

FRIAR FRANCIS If either of you know any inward impediment why you
should not be conjoined, I charge you on your souls to utter it.

CLAUDIO Know you any, Hero? 10

HERO None, my lord.

FRIAR FRANCIS Know you any, count?

LEONATO I dare make his answer, none.

CLAUDIO Oh what men dare do! What men may do! What men daily
do, not knowing what they do! 15

BENEDICK How now! Interjections? Why then, some be of laughing, as,
ah, ha, he.

CLAUDIO Stand thee by, friar: father, by your leave,
Will you with free and unconstrainèd soul
Give me this maid your daughter? 20

LEONATO As freely, son, as God did give her me.

CLAUDIO And what have I to give you back, whose worth
May counterpoise this rich and precious gift?

DON PEDRO Nothing, unless you render her again.

CLAUDIO Sweet prince, you learn me noble thankfulness. 25
There, Leonato, take her back again,
Give not this rotten orange to your friend,
She's but the sign and semblance of her honour:
Behold how like a maid she blushes here!
Oh what authority and show of truth 30
Can cunning sin cover itself withal!

[Handwritten annotations: "Claudio reacts badly to articles in love"; "He never asks Hero for her side"; "He humiliates her infront of everyone"; "Rotten"; "Unfaithful Metaphor"]

Claudio declares that he will not marry Hero. Leonato assumes that Hero has lost her virginity to Claudio, but Claudio denies this. Don Pedro denounces Hero as a common prostitute.

---

1 Speak your thoughts (in groups of about six)

Take a part each and read lines 18–88. As you finish each speech, express in a few words the emotions your character feels at that moment. For example, at some point Leonato might be 'anxious and puzzled', Hero 'scared and confused', Claudio 'savagely angry', and Don John 'excited and delighted'. Do this activity several times and see if your reactions/emotions change.

What arguments can you put forward to explain or justify Claudio and Don Pedro's public humiliation of Hero and her father?

2 Who's who and what do they know?

Don John claims to 'know' the truth (line 61). Hero is unchaste. What do the others present 'know' or believe they 'know'?

- Who's who in the picture?
- Who knows what is true, and who believes what *seems* to be true?
- Which of those with mistaken beliefs do you sympathise with?

---

luxurious lustful
approvèd wanton proven whore
known had sex with
extenuate . . . sin find an excuse for my sin of taking her virginity
large improper
comely appropriate, fitting

Dian Diana, the cool goddess of chastity and the moon
blown come into full bloom
intemperate unrestrained
Venus goddess of sexual love
wide mistakenly, wide of the mark
stale prostitute

Comes not that blood, as modest evidence,
To witness simple virtue? Would you not swear
All you that see her, that she were a maid,
By these exterior shows? But she is none: 35
She knows the heat of a luxurious bed:
Her blush is guiltiness, not modesty.

she's had sex

LEONATO What do you mean, my lord?

CLAUDIO   Not to be married,
Not to knit my soul to an approvèd wanton.   40

*where.
proven
slut.*

LEONATO Dear my lord, if you in your own proof,
Have vanquished the resistance of her youth,
And made defeat of her virginity –

CLAUDIO I know what you would say: if I have known her,
You will say, she did embrace me as a husband,
And so extenuate the forehand sin: no, Leonato,   45
I never tempted her with word too large,
But as a brother to his sister, showed
Bashful sincerity, and comely love.

HERO And seemed I ever otherwise to you?

CLAUDIO Out on thee seeming, I will write against it!   50
You seem to me as Dian in her orb,
As chaste as is the bud ere it be blown:
But you are more intemperate in your blood,
Than Venus, or those pampered animals,
That rage in savage sensuality.   55

HERO Is my lord well, that he doth speak so wide?

LEONATO Sweet prince, why speak not you?

DON PEDRO   What should I speak?
I stand dishonoured that have gone about
To link my dear friend to a common stale.

LEONATO Are these things spoken, or do I but dream?   60

DON JOHN Sir, they are spoken, and these things are true.

BENEDICK This looks not like a nuptial.

HERO   True, oh God!

CLAUDIO Leonato, stand I here?
Is this the prince? Is this the prince's brother?
Is this face Hero's? Are our eyes our own?   65

LEONATO All this is so, but what of this, my lord?

Claudio questions Hero about the man he saw at her window. Hero denies there was any man. Don Pedro and his brother confirm the truth of Claudio's accusation.

1 'Oh God defend me, how am I beset!' (in groups of five)

To show how the men, including Hero's own father, unite against her, take a part each, stand in a circle and slowly read aloud lines 63–92. Point at characters and use gesture or movement to emphasise relevant words. Here is an example using Claudio's words in line 67:

> Let me (*point to self*) but move one question (*gesture*) to your (*point to Leonato*) daughter (*point to Hero*) . . .

2 'Answer truly to your name'

The first question in the Christian catechism (a series of questions testing knowledge of the Christian faith) is 'What is your name?' In Shakespeare's time, the name Hero would have suggested faithfulness in love. In Greek legend, Hero was the true love of Leander, who drowned whilst swimming across the Hellespont to meet her. She in turn drowned herself for love of him.

Use this information to write a paragraph explaining the dialogue between Hero and Claudio (lines 72–6).

3 Claudio's farewell to Hero (in small groups)

Read aloud lines 93–101 several times. How many examples of word patterns and wordplay can you find? Look especially for **oxymorons** (two contradictory ideas placed side by side), for example Claudio's use of 'pure/impure' and 'pious/impious' contrasts.

What do you think of Claudio as he says farewell to his intended bride?

4 'Hath no man's dagger here a point for me?' [*Hero faints*]

Explain how this line might be the last straw for the beleaguered Hero.

---

kindly power   natural authority
catechising   questioning (see above)
Hero itself   the very name Hero (which he had heard Borachio speak)
no maiden   no virgin
grievèd   wronged, aggrieved
liberal   gross, coarse

much misgovernment   most serious misconduct
counsels   secret intentions
conjecture   suspicion
never . . . gracious   it (beauty) will never again be pleasing

CLAUDIO Let me but move one question to your daughter,
         And by that fatherly and kindly power,
         That you have in her, bid her answer truly.
LEONATO I charge thee do so, as thou art my child.   70
HERO Oh God defend me, how am I beset!
      What kind of catechising call you this?
CLAUDIO To make you answer truly to your name.
HERO Is it not Hero? Who can blot that name
      With any just reproach?
CLAUDIO   Marry that can Hero,   75
         Hero itself can blot out Hero's virtue.
         What man was he, talked with you yesternight,
         Out at your window betwixt twelve and one?
         Now if you are a maid, answer to this.
HERO I talked with no man at that hour, my lord.   80
DON PEDRO Why then are you no maiden. Leonato,
         I am sorry you must hear: upon mine honour,
         Myself, my brother, and this grievèd count
         Did see her, hear her, at that hour last night,
         Talk with a ruffian at her chamber window,   85
         Who hath indeed most like a liberal villain,
         Confessed the vile encounters they have had
         A thousand times in secret.
DON JOHN   Fie, fie, they are
         Not to be named my lord, not to be spoke of,
         There is not chastity enough in language,   90
         Without offence to utter them: thus, pretty lady,
         I am sorry for thy much misgovernment.
CLAUDIO Oh Hero! What a hero hadst thou been,
         If half thy outward graces had been placed
         About thy thoughts and counsels of thy heart?   95
         But fare thee well, most foul, most fair, farewell
         Thou pure impiety, and impious purity,
         For thee I'll lock up all the gates of love,
         And on my eyelids shall conjecture hang,
         To turn all beauty into thoughts of harm,   100
         And never shall it more be gracious.
LEONATO Hath no man's dagger here a point for me?
                      [*Hero faints*]

Looks are deceiving

Because she's the most beautiful and she's the most fake.

Don John claims that Hero fainted because her misdeeds have been revealed. Don Pedro, Don John and Claudio leave. Beatrice fears Hero is dead. Leonato wishes her dead and regrets he ever had a daughter.

1 Why does Benedick stay?

This is a crucial moment of decision for Benedick. Should he leave with his friends or stay with Hero and Beatrice?

a List the reasons why Benedick might be tempted to leave.

b List his reasons for staying.

c Use this information to write a 'duologue' in which the two halves of Benedick's mind explain his dilemma and his decision.

2 A father's anger and shame (in small groups)

Leonato's feelings (lines 113–36) are intense. He reflects upon the love and pride he felt for Hero and the shame he feels now that her honour 'is fallen / Into a pit of ink'.

One of you is Hero, one Leonato. Sit Hero on a chair. Leonato and the rest of the group circle Hero. As Leonato addresses his unconscious daughter, the group should violently and angrily echo the 'accusing' words (e.g. 'Wherefore?', 'Cry shame', 'Do not live', 'thy shames').

Explore the speech to discover if it 'works' as a kind of conversation. Sit in a circle. Divide the speech into smaller sections, each of which makes sense on its own. One person reads a section then 'hands on' to the next person. Try to make the lines sound like Leonato's mind debating with itself.

Early productions of the play cut part of this speech to make Leonato seem more sympathetic. More recent productions have highlighted the violence of his words, so similar to Capulet's tirade against his daughter in *Romeo and Juliet* (Act 3 Scene 5, lines 149–95). Talk about how you would present Leonato's outburst.

---

how now   What's the matter?
spirits   vital powers, life force
wherefore   why
printed . . . blood   (1) revealed by her blushes (2) part of her nature
on . . . reproaches   immediately after reproaching you

Chid . . . frame?   Did I blame nature for giving me only one child?
issue   child, offspring
smirchèd   stained
mired   muddied
salt . . . season   meat was salted to prevent it going bad

BEATRICE Why how now, cousin, wherefore sink you down?
DON JOHN Come let us go: these things come thus to light,
    Smother her spirits up.
        [Exeunt Don Pedro, Don John and Claudio]
BENEDICK   How doth the lady?   105
BEATRICE Dead I think, help, uncle!
    Hero, why Hero: uncle: Signor Benedick: friar!
LEONATO Oh Fate! Take not away thy heavy hand,
    Death is the fairest cover for her shame
    That may be wished for.
BEATRICE   How now, cousin Hero?   110
FRIAR FRANCIS Have comfort, lady.
LEONATO   Dost thou look up?
FRIAR FRANCIS Yea, wherefore should she not?
LEONATO Wherefore? Why doth not every earthly thing
    Cry shame upon her? Could she here deny
    The story that is printed in her blood?   115
    Do not live, Hero, do not ope thine eyes:
    For did I think thou wouldst not quickly die,
    Thought I thy spirits were stronger than thy shames,
    Myself would on the rearward of reproaches
    Strike at thy life. Grieved I, I had but one?   120
    Chid I for that at frugal nature's frame?
    Oh one too much by thee! Why had I one?
    Why ever wast thou lovely in my eyes?
    Why had I not with charitable hand,
    Took up a beggar's issue at my gates,   125
    Who smirchèd thus, and mired with infamy,
    I might have said, no part of it is mine,
    This shame derives itself from unknown loins:
    But mine, and mine I loved, and mine I praised,
    And mine that I was proud on, mine so much,   130
    That I myself, was to myself not mine,
    Valuing of her: why she, oh she is fallen
    Into a pit of ink, that the wide sea
    Hath drops too few to wash her clean again,
    And salt too little, which may season give   135
    To her foul tainted flesh.

Benedick asks Beatrice if she had kept Hero company that night. When Beatrice says no, Leonato is immediately convinced of his daughter's guilt and wishes her dead. Friar Francis believes Hero is innocent.

1 'By noting of the lady' (in groups of four)

Beatrice trusts Hero and knows in her 'soul' (line 139) she is innocent. Other characters desperately attempt to 'know' the truth by judging or 'noting' the outward signs. Leonato and Friar Francis are two such people. Split into two pairs:

Pair One is Leonato. As you read lines 113–68, list all the outward signs you have observed in Hero and Claudio. What do these signs lead you to believe?

Pair Two is Friar Francis. List all the outward signs you have observed. What are your conclusions and why should people trust you?

Now come together and debate your findings. If you did not know the real truth, which man would you believe?

attired   wrapped up (a clothes image)
belied   falsely accused
given . . . fortune   allowed matters to go on in this way
apparitions   signs, appearances
with experimental seal   together with my experience of life

warrant . . . book   support my book-learning
divinity   status as a theologian
perjury   lying
proper nakedness   naked truth

BENEDICK Sir, sir, be patient. For my part I am so attired in wonder, I
    know not what to say.
BEATRICE Oh on my soul my cousin is belied.
BENEDICK Lady, were you her bedfellow last night?   140
BEATRICE No truly not, although until last night,
          I have this twelve month been her bedfellow.
LEONATO Confirmed, confirmed, oh that is stronger made,
          Which was before barred up with ribs of iron.
          Would the two princes lie, and Claudio lie,   145
          Who loved her so, that speaking of her foulness,
          Washed it with tears? Hence from her, let her die.
FRIAR FRANCIS Hear me a little, for I have only been
          Silent so long, and given way unto
          This course of fortune, by noting of the lady.   150
          I have marked
          A thousand blushing apparitions,
          To start into her face, a thousand innocent shames,
          In angel whiteness beat away those blushes,
          And in her eye there hath appeared a fire,   155
          To burn the errors that these princes hold
          Against her maiden truth: call me a fool,
          Trust not my reading, nor my observations,
          Which with experimental seal doth warrant
          The tenure of my book: trust not my age,   160
          My reverence, calling, nor divinity,
          If this sweet lady lie not guiltless here,
          Under some biting error.
LEONATO   Friar, it cannot be,
          Thou seest that all the grace that she hath left,
          Is that she will not add to her damnation   165
          A sin of perjury, she not denies it:
          Why seek'st thou then to cover with excuse,
          That which appears in proper nakedness?

Hero is prepared to suffer torture and death if proven guilty. Benedick begins to suspect his friends have been deceived. Leonato swears revenge if this is true. Friar Francis advises them to pretend that Hero has died.

1 Show their reactions (in groups of five)

The accusations of Claudio and the princes have left everyone in turmoil (see picture below and on p. 108).

Devise a tableau ('frozen moment') to illustrate a line or sentence from the script opposite. Show your tableau to the rest of the class. Be prepared to hold the freeze for at least thirty seconds so the others can identify each character and guess the line your group is portraying.

2 'Publish it, that she is dead indeed' (in groups of about six)

Act out the plan that Friar Francis urges Leonato to adopt (lines 193–201). One person narrates the events which the others mime. Make sure you show every part of Friar Francis's plan.

unmeet improper
Refuse me cast me out
misprision misunderstanding
have . . . bent of honour are absolutely honourable
practice contriving
frame of plotting
invention ability to plan

means wealth
reft me robbed me
To quit . . . throughly to settle scores fully
kept in hidden indoors
mourning ostentation formal show of mourning

FRIAR FRANCIS Lady, what man is he you are accused of?

HERO They know that do accuse me, I know none: 170
      If I know more of any man alive
      Than that which maiden modesty doth warrant,
      Let all my sins lack mercy. Oh my father,
      Prove you that any man with me conversed,
      At hours unmeet, or that I yesternight   175
      Maintained the change of words with any creature,
      Refuse me, hate me, torture me to death.

FRIAR FRANCIS There is some strange misprision in the princes.

BENEDICK Two of them have the very bent of honour,
      And if their wisdoms be misled in this,   180
      The practice of it lives in John the bastard,
      Whose spirits toil in frame of villainies.

LEONATO I know not: if they speak but truth of her,
      These hands shall tear her, if they wrong her honour,
      The proudest of them shall well hear of it.   185
      Time hath not yet so dried this blood of mine,
      Nor age so eat up my invention,
      Nor fortune made such havoc of my means,
      Nor my bad life reft me so much of friends,
      But they shall find, awaked in such a kind,   190
      Both strength of limb, and policy of mind,
      Ability in means, and choice of friends,
      To quit me of them throughly.

FRIAR FRANCIS   Pause awhile,
      And let my counsel sway you in this case:
      Your daughter here the princes left for dead,   195
      Let her awhile be secretly kept in,
      And publish it, that she is dead indeed:
      Maintain a mourning ostentation,
      And on your family's old monument
      Hang mournful epitaphs, and do all rites,   200
      That appertain unto a burial.

LEONATO What shall become of this? What will this do?

Friar Francis outlines what he hopes will be the healing effect on Claudio when he hears of Hero's 'death'. If his plan fails, Hero will have to enter a nunnery.

1 'On this travail look for greater birth' (in small groups)

Friar Lawrence in *Romeo and Juliet* devised a desperately dangerous scheme to help the young lovers. Here, Shakespeare again gives the Church the difficult job ('this travail') of trying to turn tragedy into something positive ('greater birth'). Friar Francis envisages four possible outcomes to his plan:

- News of Hero's death will make her accusers feel pity (lines 203–5).
- Hero's death will bring new life to Claudio's love (lines 206–29).
- Hero's death will cleanse her of her tarnished reputation (lines 230–2).
- If the plan fails, Hero can be sent to a nunnery (lines 233–6).

Read the whole speech aloud, handing on to the next person at each colon or full stop. As each person reads, the others echo any striking words and phrases. What kind of words have you echoed?

2 Friar Francis's vision of death and rebirth (in small groups)

Identify the images Friar Francis uses to make Leonato believe his plan could work but may possibly fail.

a Read lines 206–29 of Friar Francis's speech, taking a sentence each. Write down the words and images to do with birth/death.

b Then read lines 230–6 and write down the words and images that strike you most strongly. Are these words and images different?

The Friar's hopes of rebirth will be powerfully dramatised in the final act as the play moves from the darkness of denunciation into the light of reconciliation.

---

on this travail from this labour
prize . . . worth do not fully appreciate
rack stretch, exaggerate
study of imagination brooding thoughts
habit clothes

moving excitingly
liver (thought to be the seat of passion)
success the outcome
all aim all our hopes
be levelled false remain unfulfilled
sort not does not turn out

FRIAR FRANCIS Marry, this well carried, shall on her behalf,
Change slander to remorse, that is some good,
But not for that dream I on this strange course,   205
But on this travail look for greater birth:
She dying, as it must be so maintained,
Upon the instant that she was accused,
Shall be lamented, pitied, and excused
Of every hearer: for it so falls out,   210
That what we have, we prize not to the worth,
Whiles we enjoy it; but being lacked and lost,
Why then we rack the value, then we find
The virtue that possession would not show us
Whiles it was ours: so will it fare with Claudio: 215
When he shall hear she died upon his words
Th'idea of her life shall sweetly creep
Into his study of imagination,
And every lovely organ of her life,
Shall come apparelled in more precious habit,   220
More moving-delicate, and full of life,
Into the eye and prospect of his soul
Than when she lived indeed: then shall he mourn,
If ever love had interest in his liver,
And wish he had not so accusèd her: 225
No, though he thought his accusation true:
Let this be so, and doubt not but success
Will fashion the event in better shape
Than I can lay it down in likelihood.
But if all aim but this be levelled false,   230
The supposition of the lady's death,
Will quench the wonder of her infamy.
And if it sort not well, you may conceal her,
As best befits her wounded reputation,
In some reclusive and religious life,   235
Out of all eyes, tongues, minds and injuries.

Benedick advises Leonato to accept Friar Francis's advice and promises secrecy. Alone with Beatrice, he asks how he can help to prove Hero's innocence and tells Beatrice that he loves her.

1 Hero's exit

Read lines 237–47 focusing on Hero. Write notes on how Friar Francis and Leonato behave towards her, how she responds and then leaves.

2 A crisis too for Beatrice and Benedick (in pairs)

A crisis often brings out people's real feelings (you will recall Leonato's treatment of his daughter earlier in this scene). Sit facing each other and read lines 248–316.

a **Was Don Pedro right?** Don Pedro thought Beatrice and Benedick's next meeting would be hilarious, but what qualities have they revealed in the crisis? Page 126 shows how one production staged this moment.

b **A gentler Beatrice?** Note which phrases show a gentler Beatrice with her defences down and which phrases show the old battling Beatrice with her defences up. Can you see any reasons for Beatrice's change of attitude?

c **'Not yours'** says Beatrice in line 258, meaning that it is not Benedick's duty to defend Hero, even though such a man would earn her love. Why might Beatrice believe that Benedick is not the man to challenge Claudio?

d **'As strange as the thing I know not'** No one is quite sure what Beatrice means by line 261. Try out various ways of speaking lines 261–4 and decide what you think she means. Is it a declaration of love?

---

inwardness close attachment
deal in this act in this affair
Being that . . . grief since I am
 overwhelmed with my grief
presently away let us leave at once
to strange . . . cure desperate
 diseases require desperate remedies

but prolonged simply postponed
I will not desire that I do not want you
 to do that
right her prove her innocence
even straightforward
office task, job

BENEDICK Signor Leonato, let the friar advise you,
        And though you know my inwardness and love
        Is very much unto the prince and Claudio,
        Yet, by mine honour, I will deal in this,   240
        As secretly and justly as your soul
        Should with your body.
LEONATO   Being that I flow in grief,
        The smallest twine may lead me.
FRIAR FRANCIS 'Tis well consented, presently away:
        For to strange sores, strangely they strain the cure: 245
        Come, lady, die to live, this wedding day
        Perhaps is but prolonged: have patience and endure.
                    Exeunt [Friar Francis, Leonato and Hero]
BENEDICK Lady Beatrice, have you wept all this while?
BEATRICE Yea, and I will weep a while longer.
BENEDICK I will not desire that.   250
BEATRICE You have no reason, I do it freely.
BENEDICK Surely I do believe your fair cousin is wronged.
BEATRICE Ah, how much might the man deserve of me that would right
        her!
BENEDICK Is there any way to show such friendship?   255
BEATRICE A very even way, but no such friend.
BENEDICK May a man do it?
BEATRICE It is a man's office, but not yours.

straight faced.
honest.

BENEDICK I do love nothing in the world so well as you, is not that
        strange?   260
BEATRICE As strange as the thing I know not: it were as possible for me
        to say, I loved nothing so well as you, but believe me not, and yet I
        lie not, I confess nothing, nor I deny nothing: I am sorry for my
        cousin.

Does not love anything maemanher.

115

Beatrice reluctantly admits that she loves Benedick. He swears he will do anything to prove his love for her, but refuses her order to kill Claudio. Beatrice wishes she were a man so she could take revenge herself.

1 A crucial test of love (in pairs)

Beatrice risks losing Benedick's love when she asks him to challenge his friend Claudio. He in turn risks his very life if he accepts. What Don Pedro began as an amusing 'sport' is sport no longer.

a **Freeze frames** Create six 'frozen moments' (one for each sentence in lines 278–84) which capture the emotions and intentions of Beatrice and Benedick. Show them in sequence to another pair.

b **'Kill Claudio' (line 279)** Suddenly Benedick realises the price he must pay for Beatrice's love. How might Beatrice say it and how might Benedick respond? Do *you* think he should kill Claudio?

c **Find their changing moods** Experiment with different ways of saying each line on the opposite page. Try speaking line 265 in different ways (e.g. assertively, fondly, excitedly). Then switch roles and try line 266. Continue through to line 295. Talk about your findings.

2 Eating words, eating swords, eating hearts

Now, even the wordplay becomes deadly serious. When Benedick swears by his sword (line 265), Beatrice warns him not to 'swear and eat it' (meaning 'do not go back on your oath' or perhaps 'do not eat your sword by getting yourself wounded in combat').

Identify the wordplay on the opposite page to do with swearing/ protesting love and eating words/swords. Work out how it encourages Beatrice to ask Benedick to kill Claudio. Write a paragraph on how your study of this wordplay helps you decide how Beatrice might say her final sentence (line 295).

By my sword a gentleman's last resort in the defence of honour
protest (lines 270, 273) swear
stayed . . . hour given me support at a fortunate moment
protest (line 277) object
Tarry wait, don't go

Is a not is he not
approved . . . villain proved to be the greatest villain
bear her in hand hide his real intentions
unmitigated rancour uncontrolled hatred

BENEDICK By my sword, Beatrice, thou lovest me. 265

Don't take than back → trust issues

BEATRICE Do not swear and eat it.

BENEDICK I will swear by it that you love me, and I will make him eat it that says I love not you.

BEATRICE Will you not eat your word?

BENEDICK With no sauce that can be devised to it: I protest I love thee. 270

He won't. Not tempted.

BEATRICE Why then God forgive me.

BENEDICK What offence, sweet Beatrice?

BEATRICE You have stayed me in a happy hour, I was about to protest I loved you.

BENEDICK And do it with all thy heart. 275

BEATRICE I love you with so much of my heart, that none is left to protest.

BENEDICK Come bid me do anything for thee.

To prove his love.

BEATRICE Kill Claudio.

BENEDICK Ha, not for the wide world. 280

BEATRICE You kill me to deny it, farewell.

BENEDICK Tarry, sweet Beatrice.

Thinks she's joking

BEATRICE I am gone, though I am here, there is no love in you, nay, I pray you let me go.

BENEDICK Beatrice. 285

BEATRICE In faith I will go.

BENEDICK We'll be friends first.

BEATRICE You dare easier be friends with me, than fight with mine enemy.

BENEDICK Is Claudio thine enemy? 290

BEATRICE Is a not approved in the height a villain, that hath slandered, scorned, dishonoured my kinswoman? Oh that I were a man! What, bear her in hand, until they come to take hands, and then with public accusation, uncovered slander, unmitigated rancour? Oh God that I were a man! I would eat his heart in the market place. 295

Humiliated her cousing
↓
Wands revenge.

Beatrice despairs of finding a man brave enough to take up her cause. Benedick is convinced by her belief that Hero has been wronged and determines to challenge Claudio.

1 Changing relationships of power (in pairs)

Even Beatrice is forced to realise her limitations. Three times in this scene she wishes she were a man, because only a man can challenge Claudio to single combat.

Discover how the initiative moves from Beatrice to Benedick. Place two chairs facing each other. Beatrice stands in front of her chair, Benedick sits on his. Read lines 296–316. At every colon or full stop Benedick attempts to stand up, but Beatrice pushes him down again if she feels angry enough. Decide where Benedick becomes determined enough to push Beatrice onto her chair and take control.

a proper saying a likely story	**curtsies** courtly gestures
undone ruined	**trim** smooth, insincere, glib
counties counts	**with wishing** simply by wishing
a goodly count a fine accusation	**this hand** (Whose hand does he
Count Comfect Count Candy	indicate in line 308? In line 314?)
for his sake so I could take	**render . . . account** pay dearly for
him on	what he has done

BENEDICK Hear me, Beatrice.

BEATRICE Talk with a man out at a window, a proper saying.

BENEDICK Nay, but Beatrice.

BEATRICE Sweet Hero, she is wronged, she is slandered, she is undone.

BENEDICK Beat – *→ cuts him of* · 300

BEATRICE Princes and counties! Surely a princely testimony, a goodly
count, Count Comfect, a sweet gallant surely, oh that I wcre a man
for his sake! Or that I had any friend would be a man for my sake!
But manhood is melted into curtsies, valour into compliment, and
men are only turned into tongue, and trim ones too: he is now as 305
valiant as Hercules, that only tells a lie, and swears it: I cannot be a
man with wishing, therefore I will die a woman with grieving.

BENEDICK Tarry, good Beatrice, by this hand I love thee. *prove me your love.*

BEATRICE Use it for my love some other way than swearing by it.

Wait BENEDICK Think you in your soul the Count Claudio hath wronged 310
Hero?

BEATRICE Yea, as sure as I have a thought, or a soul. *His going to do it*

BENEDICK Enough, I am engaged, I will challenge him. I will kiss your
hand, and so I leave you: by this hand, Claudio shall render me a
dear account: as you hear of me, so think of me: go comfort your 315
cousin, I must say she is dead, and so farewell.

[*Exeunt*]

*when Benedicks
love is tasted
it stays strong.*

*Agrees to
do it.*

*obstacle in no
way but...*

*shows love and trust
towards her
gives her the
benifit of the
doubt.*

119

Dogberry, Verges and the Sexton take evidence from Borachio and Conrade.
Dogberry commences his blundering cross-examination.

---

1 Dogberry has a cunning plan! (in groups of about eight)

Will Dogberry and Verges be up to the task of bringing the truth to
light? Set up your magistrate's court. Act out your version of this all-
important examination of the villains (lines 1–55). Points to consider:

- What is the 'clever' piece of legal trickery Dogberry uses to catch
  out Borachio and Conrade (lines 16–27)?
- Only the Sexton seems to know how to conduct a trial properly.
  Decide how and where he has to intervene to keep matters on track.
- Dogberry calls Conrade 'sirrah' (line 11), a customary way of
  addressing servants. How do he and Borachio react to being ordered
  about by such socially inferior imbeciles?

Identify the characters of Dogberry, Verges, Borachio, Conrade and the Sexton
from this 1996 RSC production.

Sexton a minor church official
dissembly he means 'assembly'
malefactors offenders, criminals
exhibition he means 'permission'
sirrah (see Activity 1 above)
we hope we believe so

God defend God forbid
knaves rogues
it . . . shortly it will soon be generally
  believed so
go about with get the better of
in a tale telling the same story

Act 4 Scene 2
Messina A courtroom

Enter the Constables DOGBERRY and VERGES and the SEXTON as
Town Clerk in gowns, CONRADE and BORACHIO

DOGBERRY Is our whole dissembly appeared?

VERGES Oh a stool and a cushion for the sexton.

SEXTON Which be the malefactors?

DOGBERRY Marry that am I, and my partner.

VERGES Nay that's certain, we have the exhibition to examine. 5

SEXTON But which are the offenders, that are to be examined? Let them
    come before master constable.

DOGBERRY Yea marry, let them come before me: what is your name,
    friend?

BORACHIO Borachio. 10

DOGBERRY Pray write down Borachio. Yours, sirrah?

CONRADE I am a gentleman, sir, and my name is Conrade.

DOGBERRY Write down Master Gentleman Conrade: masters, do you
    serve God?

BORACHIO   } Yea, sir, we hope. 15
CONRADE

DOGBERRY Write down, that they hope they serve God. and write God
    first, for God defend but God should go before such villains: mas-
    ters, it is proved already that you are little better than false knaves,
    and it will go near to be thought so shortly: how answer you for
    yourselves? 20

CONRADE Marry, sir, we say we are none.

DOGBERRY A marvellous witty fellow I assure you, but I will go about
    with him: come you hither, sirrah, a word in your ear, sir: I say to
    you, it is thought you are false knaves.

BORACHIO Sir, I say to you, we are none. 25

DOGBERRY Well, stand aside, 'fore God they are both in a tale: have you
    writ down, that they are none?

The Sexton instructs Dogberry to summon the Watch, who confirm that they overheard Borachio confess his crime. The Sexton reveals that Hero has since died and Don John secretly fled.

1 The Sexton's notes – with candid comments

Some regard the Sexton as the real hero of the play! Think about the part he plays in this scene and write the personal notes you think he would make at the conclusion of these proceedings (lines 1–55).

Include in your writing the Sexton's frank opinions of the other characters, including those mentioned but not present. For example, what would his opinion be of Don John?

2 How should the villains react? (in groups of three)

Focus on how Conrade and Borachio behave as the Sexton tells the news of Hero's death and Prince John's sudden departure from Messina (lines 51–5). One person speaks as the Sexton, the others respond as follows:

First response The two hard-hearted villains react unfeelingly to the news. Adopt a callous attitude and improvise what they might secretly say to each other.

Second response A villain with a conscience. In this version Borachio, unlike Conrade, is worried and guilt-stricken by the news. Show this moment and let Borachio explain why he is struck by remorse. Improvise the secret dialogue of Conrade and Borachio after they hear the Sexton's news.

Despite coming near to tragedy, the play is a comedy and will end in some kind of reconciliation. Talk together about how you would want to present your villains if you were directing the play.

---

you go . . . to examine you aren't examining properly
eftest A Dogberry invention! He may mean 'deftest' (most skilful)
flat perjury downright lying
burglary he may mean 'bribery'

by mass by the Holy Mass (a mild oath)
upon his words on the strength of (Don John's) words
redemption he means 'damnation'
upon the grief as a result of her grief

SEXTON Master constable, you go not the way to examine, you must call
  forth the watch that are their accusers.

DOGBERRY Yea marry, that's the eftest way, let the watch come forth.   30

  [*Enter* SEACOAL, WATCHMAN 2 *and the rest of the Watch*]

  Masters, I charge you in the prince's name, accuse these men.

SEACOAL This man said, sir, that Don John the prince's brother was a
  villain.

DOGBERRY Write down, Prince John a villain: why this is flat perjury, to
  call a prince's brother villain.   35

BORACHIO Master constable.

DOGBERRY Pray thee, fellow, peace, I do not like thy look I promise
  thee.

SEXTON What heard you him say else?

WATCHMAN 2 Marry that he had received a thousand ducats of Don   40
  John, for accusing the Lady Hero wrongfully.

DOGBERRY Flat burglary as ever was committed.

VERGES Yea by mass that it is.

SEXTON What else, fellow?

SEACOAL And that Count Claudio did mean upon his words, to dis-   45
  grace Hero before the whole assembly, and not marry her.

DOGBERRY Oh villain! Thou wilt be condemned into everlasting
  redemption for this.

SEXTON What else?

SEACOAL This is all.   50

SEXTON And this is more, masters, than you can deny: Prince John is
  this morning secretly stolen away: Hero was in this manner accused,
  in this very manner refused, and upon the grief of this, suddenly
  died: master constable, let these men be bound, and brought to
  Leonato's: I will go before and show him their examination. [*Exit*]   55

As the Watch escort the prisoners away, Conrade offers some resistance. Exasperated beyond endurance, he calls Dogberry an ass, an insult which mortally offends Dogberry.

---

1 How much of 'an ass' is Dogberry? (in small groups)

Dogberry has been called an ass, but there is no one left able to write it down as evidence. It is an insult that still rankles with Dogberry when next we see him!

a Smugly certain of his own worth? Two of you read the parts of Dogberry and Conrade (lines 57–71). When Dogberry speaks, Conrade leads the rest of the group in mockingly echoing what the Master Constable says. Dogberry should be angrily pompous in response to this.

b Strangely sympathetic? Decide whether Dogberry deserves some sympathy (some productions have tried to create this effect). Dogberry is obviously sensitive about his position and prestige. For example, he boasts about having two gowns (gowns were expensive and a mark of affluence and authority). When Dogberry and Conrade speak lines 57–71, the others must echo and comment in support of Dogberry, who should respond to their sympathy.

2 Present your comic double act (in pairs)

Comedy lies as much in expression, mannerisms and movement as it does in the words. You will by now have formed your own picture of Dogberry and Verges. Choose one character each. Find a short phrase from lines 1–71 typical of your character. Memorise it.

Each pair then gives their physical 'illustration' of these two men as they huff and puff about the room, repeating their memorised lines/phrases. Switch roles/lines and repeat.

---

opinioned he means 'pinioned' (bound)
coxcomb conceited fool
God's my life a mild oath
naughty wicked, worthless (a much stronger meaning than today)

varlet rogue, low fellow
suspect he means 'respect'
piety he means 'impiety' (wickedness)
go to I'll have you know
had losses lost money (but survived)
writ down recorded

VERGES Come, let them be opinioned.

CONRADE Let them be in the hands of coxcomb.

DOGBERRY God's my life, where's the sexton? Let him write down the prince's officer coxcomb: come, bind them, thou naughty varlet.

CONRADE Away, you are an ass, you are an ass.   60

DOGBERRY Dost thou not suspect my place? Dost thou not suspect my years? Oh that he were here to write me down an ass! But masters, remember that I am an ass, though it be not written down, yet forget not that I am an ass: no, thou villain, thou art full of piety as shall be proved upon thee by good witness: I am a wise fellow, and which is   65
more, an officer, and which is more, a householder, and which is more, as pretty a piece of flesh as any is in Messina, and one that knows the law, go to, and a rich fellow enough, go to, and a fellow that hath had losses, and one that hath two gowns, and everything handsome about him: bring him away: oh that I had been writ down   70
an ass!

Exeunt

Looking back at Act 4
Activities for groups or individuals

1 Beatrice – caught up in a whirlwind

As the play's double plot comes to a double crisis, Beatrice finds herself at the centre of both. She had probably anticipated the wedding would be a difficult time for her. She had been 'exceeding ill' that morning and faced her first meeting with Benedick since learning of his love for her. However, she could not possibly have foreseen the shocks in store for them both.

a Quickly note down a chronological list of what happens to Beatrice in Act 4. After each item, write what you think Beatrice is feeling.

b Form a small group and compile a joint list using all your best ideas. Use this to prepare a 'Beatrice-monologue' in which you take turns to narrate Beatrice's version of the events at the church. The picture below and those on pages 110 and 118 may help you.

c Present your version to the class. Be inventive. Think about how you might share the lines, speak as a chorus, echo, or mime to show her emotions.

Benedick attempts to comfort a distraught Beatrice.

2 Benedick's moments of decision

Benedick is almost as shaken by the events of Act 4 Scene 1 as Beatrice. Devise a way of showing the changes in his emotions, perhaps by means of a graph or chart, or through a series of cartoons with captions. Two of you could show the changes dramatically with one person naming the mood, and the other showing it.

3 Wounded male pride

Look back at Dogberry's comic display of wounded pride (Act 4 Scene 2, lines 61–71). Claudio's speeches (Act 4 Scene 1, lines 25–101) are more serious outpourings of wounded vanity. Read what both men say. Make notes on:

- what motivates each man to say what he does
- how the language of each man differs
- which of the two men you have more sympathy for, and why.

4 The silent Hero speaks

Imagine Hero has been placed in a nunnery. There, she gives a frank account of what happened to her at the wedding. What would she say? Have her talk about her hopes before the wedding, what happened at the church, what she now thinks of Claudio, Don Pedro and Leonato, and how she views her present situation.

5 Outward signs and inner truths

Many characters try to judge inner truth by outward signs. Leonato, Don Pedro, Claudio and the Friar have all 'noted' different things about Hero. Leonato 'notes' Claudio's tears (Act 4 Scene 1, line 147), which *he* interprets as a sign of the young man's sincerity. In Scene 2, Dogberry lists all the outward signs of his own dignity and wealth.

Find a way of presenting these ideas about outward signs and inner truths to the class. This might be as a diagram, a comic strip with captions, as columns headed 'Truth' and 'Signs' – or some other visual presentation.

6 News!

You are a reporter sent to cover either (1) the wedding of Leonato's daughter to the famous war hero, Count Claudio, or (2) the trial of two drunken gentlemen arrested by the local Watch. Your paper could be either a scandal-mongering publication or a more sober and thoughtful one.

Antonio attempts to console his brother, but the loss of his daughter's reputation continues to hit Leonato hard. Only a man who has suffered as he has is entitled to offer him counsel.

1 Feel the darkness of Leonato's grief (in groups of three)

The play has come very close to tragedy. Leonato expresses his feelings of grief (lines 3–32) in three sections:

- Only the man who has loved and suffered can rightfully talk of patience and endurance (lines 3–19).
- But there is no such man. When a man feels grief, all thoughts of patience and endurance are immediately forgotten (lines 20–6).
- All men can preach patience to those who suffer, but no one can practise what they preach when sorrow comes to them (lines 27–32).

Take a section each and practise reading it to yourself with as much anguish as you can. Then come back together and read the lines in sequence expressing your grief.

2 Is Leonato self-indulgent? (in small groups)

Some directors have cut parts of Leonato's speech (lines 3–32), possibly feeling his grief to be overly 'tragic'. Decide what is Leonato's most self-indulgent phrase or sentence and explain your choice to the rest of the group. Keep in mind the following points when coming to your decision:

- Has anything happened at the wedding to make you somewhat sceptical about Leonato's love for his daughter and his current sense of loss?
- Messina is a patriarchal (male-dominated) society with male values (honour, allegiance and so on). Might you therefore sympathise with Leonato's anguish at Hero's ruined reputation?

---

second add yet more
suit match
lineament feature
wag look foolish
cry hem cough uncertainly
make . . . wasters drown sorrow by studying late into the night

preceptial medicine moral instruction
'tis . . . office everyone thinks they can
wring writhe with pain
sufficiency ability
advertisement advice offered

Act 5 Scene 1
Outside Leonato's house

Enter LEONATO and his brother ANTONIO

ANTONIO If you go on thus, you will kill yourself,
       And 'tis not wisdom thus to second grief,
       Against yourself.
LEONATO   I pray thee cease thy counsel,
       Which falls into mine ears as profitless,
       As water in a sieve: give not me counsel,   5
       Nor let no comforter delight mine ear,
       But such a one whose wrongs do suit with mine.
       Bring me a father that so loved his child,
       Whose joy of her is overwhelmed like mine,
       And bid him speak of patience,   10
       Measure his woe the length and breadth of mine,
       And let it answer every strain for strain,
       As thus for thus, and such a grief for such,
       In every lineament, branch, shape and form:
       If such a one will smile and stroke his beard,   15
       And sorrow; wag, cry hem, when he should groan;
       Patch grief with proverbs, make misfortune drunk
       With candle-wasters: bring him yet to me,
       And I of him will gather patience:
       But there is no such man, for, brother, men   20
       Can counsel and speak comfort to that grief,
       Which they themselves not feel, but tasting it,
       Their counsel turns to passion, which before,
       Would give preceptial medicine to rage,
       Fetter strong madness in a silken thread,   25
       Charm ache with air, and agony with words –
       No, no, 'tis all men's office, to speak patience
       To those that wring under the load of sorrow,
       But no man's virtue nor sufficiency
       To be so moral, when he shall endure   30
       The like himself: therefore give me no counsel,
       My griefs cry louder than advertisement.

As Leonato's mind turns to thoughts of revenge, the sight of Claudio and Don Pedro hurrying past, apparently unconcerned about the grief they have caused him, quickly arouses his anger.

---

1 Feelings are running high (in groups of four)

There are many powerful outbursts in this scene. Present lines 27–57 in a way that highlights the swift changes of mood.

Consider the way in which Leonato and Antonio talk together, the manner of Don Pedro and Claudio's entrance, how each reacts on seeing Leonato, and the response of the two old men. Decide how to emphasise the meaning of Leonato's remarks in lines 47–57.

2 Philosophers and the toothache

Leonato says in lines 35–8 that philosophers have spoken very dismissively about how hard it is to endure pain and misfortune ('made a push at chance and sufferance'), but when they are put to the test themselves (i.e. when they have to 'endure the tooth-ache'), they can't practise what they preach.

Draw a cartoon which illustrates the meaning of Leonato's image.

3 'Thou dissembler, thou' (in pairs)

You will remember how Leonato addressed his guests in the opening scene of the play using the polite 'you' form. Use of the 'thou' form is a sign of friendship, but it can also signal contempt (see p. 166).

Take it in turns to tell Claudio what you think of him (lines 52–7, from 'Who wrongs him?' onwards). Stress all the 'thee/thou' words. Try it in different ways, mockingly, smilingly or angrily. Afterwards, discuss how this explains Claudio's actions at line 54.

However   however much
writ . . . gods   written with a god-like superiority
made a push at   looked with contempt on
sufferance   suffering
bend   turn

belied   falsely accused
all is one   it doesn't matter now
lie low   have to watch out
dissembler   deceiver
beshrew   a curse on
nothing to   nothing in moving to

ANTONIO Therein do men from children nothing differ.
LEONATO I pray thee peace, I will be flesh and blood,
      For there was never yet philosopher,   35
      That could endure the tooth-ache patiently,
      However they have writ the style of gods,
      And made a push at chance and sufferance.
ANTONIO Yet bend not all the harm upon yourself,
      Make those that do offend you suffer too.   40
LEONATO There thou speak'st reason, nay I will do so,
      My soul doth tell me, Hero is belied,
      And that shall Claudio know, so shall the prince,
      And all of them that thus dishonour her.

Enter DON PEDRO *and* CLAUDIO

ANTONIO Here comes the prince and Claudio hastily.   45
DON PEDRO Good den, good den.
CLAUDIO   Good day to both of you.
LEONATO Hear you, my lords?
DON PEDRO   We have some haste, Leonato.
LEONATO Some haste, my lord! Well, fare you well, my lord,
      Are you so hasty now? Well, all is one.
DON PEDRO Nay do not quarrel with us, good old man.   50
ANTONIO If he could right himself with quarrelling,
      Some of us would lie low.
CLAUDIO   Who wrongs him?
LEONATO Marry thou dost wrong me, thou dissembler, thou:
      Nay, never lay thy hand upon thy sword,
      I fear thee not.
CLAUDIO   Marry beshrew my hand,   55
      If it should give your age such cause of fear,
      In faith my hand meant nothing to my sword.

Despite his age, Leonato challenges Claudio to single combat, but Claudio refuses to fight a duel with the old man. Then Antonio challenges Claudio so fiercely that even Leonato is surprised.

1 Challenges and responses (in groups of four)

Stand face to face, Leonato and Antonio opposite Claudio and Don Pedro. Read aloud lines 58–90. Gesture vigorously as you speak your lines. Leonato and Antonio could prod Claudio firmly with their fingers on each relevant word (e.g. 'Claudio', 'thy', 'thee', 'Sir Boy', 'braggarts') and pat their own chests when referring to themselves.

Decide how Claudio and Don Pedro should respond to this aggression. Are they surprised, amused, hostile, sneering, unnerved?

A laughing Claudio faces Antonio's challenge as Leonato and Don Pedro watch.

fleer smile contemptuously	**active practice** training
dotard senile old man	**lustihood** physical fitness
to thy head to your face	**daff me** brush me aside
trial of a man single combat	**foining** thrusting (fencing term)
never . . . slept never before has any disgrace been buried	**Content yourself** wait a minute
	apes fools
nice fence skilful swordsmanship	**Jacks** rogues

LEONATO Tush, tush, man, never fleer and jest at me,
        I speak not like a dotard, nor a fool,
        As under privilege of age to brag,   60
        What I have done, being young, or what would do,
        Were I not old: know, Claudio, to thy head,
        Thou hast so wronged mine innocent child and me,
        That I am forced to lay my reverence by,
        And with grey hairs and bruise of many days,   65
        Do challenge thee to trial of a man:
        I say thou hast belied mine innocent child.
        Thy slander hath gone through and through her heart,
        And she lies buried with her ancestors:
        Oh in a tomb where never scandal slept,   70
        Save this of hers, framed by thy villainy.
CLAUDIO My villainy?
LEONATO   Thine, Claudio, thine I say.
DON PEDRO You say not right, old man.
LEONATO   My lord, my lord,
        I'll prove it on his body if he dare,
        Despite his nice fence, and his active practice,   75
        His May of youth, and bloom of lustihood.
CLAUDIO Away, I will not have to do with you.
LEONATO Canst thou so daff me? Thou hast killed my child,
        If thou kill'st me, boy, thou shalt kill a man.
ANTONIO He shall kill two of us, and men indeed,   80
        But that's no matter, let him kill one first:
        Win me and wear me, let him answer me,
        Come follow me, boy, come, Sir Boy, come follow me,
        Sir Boy, I'll whip you from your foining fence,
        Nay, as I am a gentleman, I will.
LEONATO   Brother.   85
ANTONIO Content yourself, God knows, I loved my niece,
        And she is dead, slandered to death by villains,
        That dare as well answer a man indeed,
        As I dare take a serpent by the tongue.
        Boys, apes, braggarts, Jacks, milksops.
LEONATO   Brother Anthony.   90

Don Pedro maintains his belief that Claudio was correct in his accusation of Hero. As the two old men depart, still rumbling angrily, a grimly determined Benedick arrives on the scene.

---

1 Claudio in the line of fire

Antonio (lines 91–8) sees Claudio as one of those shallow, worthless fashion-conscious young men that Borachio so despises (Act 3 Scene 3, lines 107–13). Can you defend the young war hero's behaviour in this scene? Look at how he conducts himself with first Leonato, then Antonio and finally Benedick (lines 45–121).

First list the accusations that the three men might make against him. Next, list the things that Claudio might say in his defence. Write a paragraph giving your own views on which parts of each side's case you can accept.

2 'I came to seek you both' (in groups of five)

Benedick has also come to challenge Claudio and his intentions are deadly serious. Rehearse your version of lines 91–121 and consider the following:

The impotent rage of two old men (lines 91–107) How much 'ancient fury' can your Antonio summon up? But think also how ludicrous it is for an old man to attack a proven fighter like Claudio. The others will need to consider how they can help to convey this combination of fury and ridiculousness.

Benedick's entrance – a real threat (lines 109–21) Think about the dramatic pause between the exits and this entrance, how Don Pedro and Claudio react as their friend enters, and how Benedick can convey his determination.

Show your version to the class and discuss with them the dramatic impact of this combination of comedy and seriousness.

---

scruple tiniest amount
Scambling unruly, arguing
out-facing conceited, swaggering
fashion-monging fashion-conscious
cog cheat
flout brag
deprave abuse people

Go anticly dress grotesquely
hideousness formidableness
durst cared to go that far
wake your patience urge you to be patient
with two by two
high proof extremely

ANTONIO Hold you content, what, man! I know them, yea
       And what they weigh, even to the utmost scruple:
       Scambling, out-facing, fashion-monging boys,
       That lie, and cog, and flout, deprave and slander,
       Go anticly, and show outward hideousness,   95
       And speak off half a dozen dangerous words,
       How they might hurt their enemies, if they durst,
       And this is all.
LEONATO But brother Anthony –
ANTONIO   Come 'tis no matter,
       Do not you meddle, let me deal in this.   100
DON PEDRO Gentlemen both, we will not wake your patience,
       My heart is sorry for your daughter's death:
       But on my honour she was charged with nothing
       But what was true, and very full of proof.
LEONATO My lord, my lord –
DON PEDRO   I will not hear you.   105
LEONATO No come, brother, away, I will be heard.
ANTONIO And shall, or some of us will smart for it.
                    Exeunt Leonato and Antonio
DON PEDRO See, see, here comes the man we went to seek.

                 Enter BENEDICK

CLAUDIO Now, signor, what news?
BENEDICK   Good day, my lord.
DON PEDRO Welcome, signor, you are almost come to part almost a   110
    fray.
CLAUDIO We had like to have had our two noses snapped off with two
    old men without teeth.
DON PEDRO Leonato and his brother: what think'st thou? Had we
    fought, I doubt we should have been too young for them.   115
BENEDICK In a false quarrel there is no true valour: I came to seek you
    both.
CLAUDIO We have been up and down to seek thee, for we are high
    proof melancholy, and would fain have it beaten away, wilt thou use
    thy wit?   120
BENEDICK It is in my scabbard, shall I draw it?

Don Pedro and Claudio welcome Benedick's arrival as much-needed light relief. The deadly serious Benedick, unmoved by their mockery, challenges Claudio for causing the death of Hero.

1 Attempts at light-heartedness (in groups of three)

Don Pedro and Claudio look to Benedick to cheer them up after their bruising encounter with Leonato and Antonio.

- Benedick's serious reference to his wit being his sword is joked about as Claudio asks him to 'draw' his wit just as a minstrel would draw pleasant music from his instrument (lines 121–4).
- Benedick then uses the fighting image of a 'career' or charge of knights in a tournament (lines 129–30). Claudio jokingly counters this by comparing Benedick to a knight who breaks his lance with a clumsy sideways blow ('give him another staff, this last was broke cross').

Take parts and read lines 118–46. At what point does the joking start to turn sour? Does Claudio realise before Don Pedro?

2 A warning signal (in groups of three)

Elizabethans might well have sensed very quickly that all was not right with Benedick. Read page 166 on the use of 'thou/you', then take a part each and read lines 122–56. Stress forcefully every 'thou/thy' and 'you/your'. Who uses which form and why? What prompts Claudio to change his manner of address during these lines?

3 Easing an awkward moment

Why does the prince tell Benedick at some length the witty remarks that Beatrice made about him (lines 147–56)? How do you imagine Benedick and Claudio react to his anecdotes?

---

beside their wit   mad
care . . . cat   a proverb
how . . . girdle   what to do about it
God bless me   God protect me
calf, capon, woodcock   all stupid, harmless animals
curiously   skilfully

fine   (1) very good (2) delicate
wise gentleman   fool
hath the tongues   speaks several languages
forswore   retracted, took back
trans-shape   distort
properest   most handsome

DON PEDRO Dost thou wear thy wit by thy side?

CLAUDIO Never any did so, though very many have been beside their wit: I will bid thee draw, as we do the minstrels, draw to pleasure us.

DON PEDRO As I am an honest man, he looks pale, art thou sick, or angry? 125

CLAUDIO What, courage, man: what though care killed a cat, thou hast mettle enough in thee to kill care.

BENEDICK Sir, I shall meet your wit in the career, and you charge it against me: I pray you choose another subject. 130

CLAUDIO Nay then, give him another staff, this last was broke cross.

DON PEDRO By this light, he changes more and more, I think he be angry indeed.

CLAUDIO If he be, he knows how to turn his girdle.

BENEDICK Shall I speak a word in your ear? 135

CLAUDIO God bless me from a challenge.

BENEDICK You are a villain, I jest not, I will make it good how you dare, with what you dare, and when you dare: do me right, or I will protest your cowardice: you have killed a sweet lady, and her death shall fall heavy on you: let me hear from you. 140

CLAUDIO Well I will meet you, so I may have good cheer.

DON PEDRO What, a feast, a feast?

CLAUDIO I'faith I thank him, he hath bid me to a calf's head and a capon, the which if I do not carve most curiously, say my knife's naught: shall I not find a woodcock too? 145

BENEDICK Sir, your wit ambles well, it goes easily.

DON PEDRO I'll tell thee how Beatrice praised thy wit the other day: I said thou hadst a fine wit, true said she, a fine little one: no said I, a great wit: right says she, a great gross one: nay said I, a good wit: just said she, it hurts nobody: nay said I, the gentleman is wise: certain 150 said she, a wise gentleman: nay said I, he hath the tongues: that I believe said she, for he swore a thing to me on Monday night, which he forswore on Tuesday morning, there's a double tongue, there's two tongues: thus did she an hour together trans-shape thy particular virtues, yet at last she concluded with a sigh, thou wast the 155 properest man in Italy.

Benedick resigns from Don Pedro's service. He informs the prince that Don John has fled and accuses his former friends of bringing about the death of Hero. Don John's men are brought in under guard.

1 Accusations (in groups of four)

Two of you speak Benedick's parting words (lines 167–73) to the other two, changing over at each colon. Then reverse roles and do it again. Try different ways of accusing your two former friends.

2 How unfeeling are Don Pedro and Claudio?

Some people find a comment Don Pedro makes on the opposite page to be unbelievably thoughtless and Claudio's response equally insensitive. Identify the comment and response and explain why people might find them so shocking.

3 Echoes

Every Shakespeare play is full of resonances. As each scene unfolds, you start to hear echoes of language that has been used before.

a **Cuckolds again** In lines 158–66 Don Pedro and Claudio hint at the trick they played on Benedick, and mock him with the cuckolded husband joke. Find the remarks Benedick made in Act 1 Scene 1 which are echoed here when Don Pedro and Claudio talk of the 'savage bull's horns' and 'Benedick the married man'. What is ironic about their jesting here when you consider what has just happened in Acts 3 and 4?

b **'Lord Lack-beard there'** List the insults that Benedick aims at Claudio in this scene. Compare them with the comments Beatrice has made about the Count (Act 2 Scene 1, lines 222–4 and Act 4 Scene 1, lines 291–307). Are there any similarities?

---

deadly until she died
braggarts boasters
among you between you
doublet and hose i.e. his usual
 clothes
giant hero
ape fool

doctor wise man
sad serious
more reasons any more evidence
balance scales
once (proved) once and for all
Hearken after enquire into

CLAUDIO For the which she wept heartily, and said she cared not.

DON PEDRO Yea that she did, but yet for all that, and if she did not hate him deadly, she would love him dearly, the old man's daughter told us all. 160

CLAUDIO All, all, and moreover, God saw him when he was hid in the garden.

DON PEDRO But when shall we set the savage bull's horns on the sensible Benedick's head?

CLAUDIO Yea and text underneath, 'Here dwells Benedick the married 165 man'?

BENEDICK Fare you well, boy, you know my mind, I will leave you now to your gossip-like humour: you break jests as braggarts do their blades, which God be thanked hurt not: my lord, for your many courtesies I thank you: I must discontinue your company: your 170 brother the bastard is fled from Messina: you have among you killed a sweet and innocent lady: for my Lord Lack-beard there, he and I shall meet, and till then peace be with him.   [*Exit*]

DON PEDRO He is in earnest.

CLAUDIO In most profound earnest, and I'll warrant you, for the love of 175 Beatrice.

DON PEDRO And hath challenged thee?

CLAUDIO Most sincerely.

DON PEDRO What a pretty thing man is, when he goes in his doublet and hose, and leaves off his wit! 180

CLAUDIO He is then a giant to an ape, but then is an ape a doctor to such a man.

DON PEDRO But soft you, let me be, pluck up my heart, and be sad, did he not say my brother was fled?

Enter DOGBERRY *and* VERGES, CONRADE *and* BORACHIO [*with Watchmen*]

DOGBERRY Come you, sir, if justice cannot tame you, she shall ne'er 185 weigh more reasons in her balance, nay, and you be a cursing hypocrite once, you must be looked to.

DON PEDRO How now, two of my brother's men bound? Borachio one.

CLAUDIO Hearken after their offence, my lord.

DON PEDRO Officers, what offence have these men done? 190

139

As Dogberry begins his repetitive and garbled account of the trial, Don Pedro questions Borachio, who immediately and shamefacedly confesses the whole plot to disgrace Hero.

1 False report, untruths, slanders and lying knaves

Again Shakespeare mingles the comic and serious. In line 199, Claudio's comment 'there's one meaning well suited' refers to Dogberry's listing of six 'differently identical' crimes, which Don Pedro cleverly mimics (lines 191–7). One baffled Dogberry swayed precariously at this point.

Step into role as director and write notes for the two actors on how to deliver this exchange to the maximum comic effect.

2 From comic to deeply serious (in groups of about eight)

Borachio follows Dogberry's garbled report with a much more profound perspective on 'false report', 'untruths', 'slanders' and 'lying knaves'.

Borachio's confession One person takes the part of Borachio, the rest take up the positions of the other characters present, including the Watch. As Borachio slowly reads lines 203–13, he points to the relevant characters (see p. 64 for an example of how to do this). Repeat, with the other characters reacting to and echoing Borachio's words. Present your version to the class.

The heart of the play? Borachio's account of how he deceived Claudio and Don Pedro is deeply perceptive. A central preoccupation of the play is the difficulty people have in distinguishing truth from illusion, appearance from reality. Talk together about what comment the following sentences have to say about this problem:

- 'I have deceived even your very eyes'
- 'what your wisdoms could not discover, these shallow fools have brought to light'
- 'you . . . saw me court Margaret in Hero's garments'.

---

in his own division i.e. divided up as Dogberry has
bound . . . answer summoned to answer charges
cunning clever
go no . . . answer answer straightaway

incensed me incited me
set thee on urge you
the practice of it carrying it out
rare semblance exquisite appearance
plaintiffs he means 'defendants'
reformed he means 'informed'

DOGBERRY Marry, sir, they have committed false report, moreover they have spoken untruths, secondarily, they are slanders, sixth and lastly, they have belied a lady, thirdly they have verified unjust things, and to conclude, they are lying knaves.

DON PEDRO First I ask thee what they have done, thirdly I ask thee what's their offence, sixth and lastly why they are committed, and to conclude, what you lay to their charge? 195

CLAUDIO Rightly reasoned, and in his own division, and by my troth there's one meaning well suited.

DON PEDRO Who have you offended, masters, that you are thus bound to your answer? This learned constable is too cunning to be understood: what's your offence? 200

BORACHIO Sweet prince, let me go no farther to mine answer: do you hear me, and let this count kill me: I have deceived even your very eyes: what your wisdoms could not discover, these shallow fools have brought to light, who in the night overheard me confessing to this man, how Don John your brother incensed me to slander the Lady Hero, how you were brought into the orchard, and saw me court Margaret in Hero's garments, how you disgraced her when you should marry her: my villainy they have upon record, which I had rather seal with my death, than repeat over to my shame: the lady is dead upon mine and my master's false accusation: and briefly I desire nothing but the reward of a villain. 205 210

DON PEDRO Runs not this speech like iron through your blood?

CLAUDIO I have drunk poison whiles he uttered it. 215

DON PEDRO But did my brother set thee on to this?

BORACHIO Yea, and paid me richly for the practice of it.

DON PEDRO He is composed and framed of treachery,
And fled he is upon this villainy.

CLAUDIO Sweet Hero, now thy image doth appear 220
In the rare semblance that I loved it first.

DOGBERRY Come, bring away the plaintiffs, by this time our sexton hath reformed Signor Leonato of the matter: and masters, do not forget to specify when time and place shall serve, that I am an ass.

VERGES Here, here comes Master Signor Leonato, and the sexton too. 225

Leonato returns. Claudio and the prince, full of remorse, beg to be able to make amends. Leonato orders Claudio to mourn Hero's death that night at her tomb and later marry his niece.

An angry Leonato turns away from Borachio to confront Claudio and Don Pedro. Which line do you think he is about to speak?

1 'And so dies my revenge' (in groups of five)

A very thin line divides Shakespearian comedy from tragedy. The outcome of this play could so easily have been different. In *Othello* (a later play), Shakespeare showed just how disastrous it could be when a man suspects his wife of having an affair.

Act out lines 226–60 in a way that shows Leonato's anger, sarcasm and vengeful feelings, but also his forgiveness and mercy. One production even made the audience laugh at line 255. Can you?

---

when I note   when I notice
beliest thyself   wrong yourself
bethink you of it   think about it
Impose . . . my sin   make me suffer
  whatever punishment you can think of
bend under   endure the burden of

enjoin   commit
Possess   inform
labour . . . invention   produce
  anything by way of a poetic tribute
Give her the right   i.e. make her your
  wife

Enter LEONATO, *his brother* [ANTONIO] *and the Sexton*

LEONATO Which is the villain? Let me see his eyes,
        That when I note another man like him,
        I may avoid him: which of these is he?
BORACHIO If you would know your wronger, look on me.
LEONATO Art thou the slave that with thy breath hast killed   230
        Mine innocent child?
BORACHIO   Yea, even I alone.
LEONATO No, not so, villain, thou beliest thyself,
        Here stand a pair of honourable men,
        A third is fled that had a hand in it:
        I thank you, princes, for my daughter's death,   235
        Record it with your high and worthy deeds,
        'Twas bravely done, if you bethink you of it.
CLAUDIO I know not how to pray your patience,
        Yet I must speak, choose your revenge yourself,
        Impose me to what penance your invention   240
        Can lay upon my sin, yet sinned I not,
        But in mistaking.
DON PEDRO   By my soul nor I,
        And yet to satisfy this good old man,
        I would bend under any heavy weight,
        That he'll enjoin me to.   245
LEONATO I cannot bid you bid my daughter live,
        That were impossible, but I pray you both,
        Possess the people in Messina here,
        How innocent she died, and if your love
        Can labour aught in sad invention,   250
        Hang her an epitaph upon her tomb,
        And sing it to her bones, sing it tonight:
        Tomorrow morning come you to my house,
        And since you could not be my son-in-law,
        Be yet my nephew: my brother hath a daughter,   255
        Almost the copy of my child that's dead,
        And she alone is heir to both of us,
        Give her the right you should have given her cousin,
        And so dies my revenge.
CLAUDIO   Oh noble sir!
        Your over kindness doth wring tears from me,   260

Borachio assures Leonato of Margaret's innocence in the whole affair. Dogberry leaves, still very much concerned that it should be recorded in writing that he has been called an ass.

---

1 Final thoughts on Dogberry (in small groups)

A scene which began on the verge of tragedy ends on a comic note. Not even a prince, a count, a governor and several signors can silence Dogberry! This is the last the audience sees of him, however. To help clarify your views about him, try the following:

a **Does Dogberry deserve to be 'writ down an ass'?** Half the group gathers evidence to support this view. The other half prepares his defence. Argue the case.

b **How does Dogberry leave?** Act out your version of Dogberry's exit (lines 271–89). Look for comic opportunities from the garbled way in which he takes his leave and the bemused reactions of Leonato and the rest. Decide how hard he has to work to get his money (line 282), and how much of it (if any) he gives to Verges. One production made a very amusing use of the missed handshake routine!

c **'The watch heard them talk of one Deformed'** In passing through the brain of Dogberry, the story of the notorious villain Deformed has achieved an amazing degree of distortion. It began in Act 3 Scene 3, where Borachio talked of 'that deformed thief fashion'. The Watchman, mistaking what he heard for an actual thief, declared that Deformed wore a lovelock (see pp. 170–1).

Dogberry is still doggedly pursuing this illusory villain, but what has his brain done to the lovelock?

2 'We'll talk with Margaret' (in pairs)

Some people have wondered why Margaret did not tell anyone that it was she who was at Hero's bedroom window. Improvise the scene in which Leonato asks Margaret to explain her behaviour.

---

embrace seize upon
dispose . . . of from now on do what you like with
naughty wicked
packed involved
by her about her

under . . . black recorded in writing
God save the foundation a beggar's phrase of thanks
look for you will expect you
lewd base, worthless

        I do embrace your offer, and dispose
        For henceforth of poor Claudio.

LEONATO Tomorrow then I will expect your coming,
        Tonight I take my leave: this naughty man
        Shall face-to-face be brought to Margaret,   265
        Who I believe was packed in all this wrong,
        Hired to it by your brother.

BORACHIO   No by my soul she was not,
        Nor knew not what she did when she spoke to me,
        But always hath been just and virtuous
        In anything that I do know by her.   270

DOGBERRY Moreover, sir, which indeed is not under white and black, this plaintiff here, the offender, did call me ass, I beseech you let it be remembered in his punishment: and also the watch heard them talk of one Deformed, they say he wears a key in his ear, and a lock hanging by it, and borrows money in God's name, the which he hath 275 used so long, and never paid, that now men grow hard hearted and will lend nothing for God's sake: pray you examine him upon that point.

LEONATO I thank thee for thy care and honest pains.

DOGBERRY Your worship speaks like a most thankful and reverent 280 youth, and I praise God for you.

LEONATO There's for thy pains.

DOGBERRY God save the foundation.

LEONATO Go, I discharge thee of thy prisoner, and I thank thee.

DOGBERRY I leave an arrant knave with your worship, which I beseech 285 your worship to correct yourself, for the example of others: God keep your worship, I wish your worship well, God restore you to health, I humbly give you leave to depart, and if a merry meeting may be wished, God prohibit it: come, neighbour.

                   Exeunt [*Dogberry and Verges*]

LEONATO Until tomorrow morning, lords, farewell.   290

ANTONIO Farewell, my lords, we look for you tomorrow.

DON PEDRO We will not fail.

CLAUDIO   Tonight I'll mourn with Hero.

             [*Exeunt Don Pedro and Claudio*]

LEONATO Bring you these fellows on, we'll talk with Margaret, how her acquaintance grew with this lewd fellow.

                   Exeunt

Benedick seeks Margaret's help in arranging a meeting with Beatrice. As he awaits Beatrice's arrival, he attempts a love song and laments his inability to express his love in rhyme.

1 A comic or sombre moment?

As she did earlier with Beatrice, Margaret attempts to match wits with Benedick in playfully bawdy language full of *double entendres* (double meanings). Sexual innuendo runs through their conversation (lines 1–17):

come over	surpass (suggesting 'take sexually')
buckler	shield (suggesting 'belly, vagina')
swords/pikes	weapons (suggesting 'penis')
vice	clamp (suggesting 'gripping thighs'?).

Margaret seems strangely unconcerned about the part she has played in Hero's slander and 'death'. Both she and Benedick would be as yet unaware of Borachio's confession.

Think about all that has happened so far and what Leonato has said will happen that night and tomorrow morning. Write director's notes on the mood you want to achieve at the beginning of this scene and how you would create it.

2 Benedick – soldier but no poet!

The ideal Elizabethan man was both soldier and poet. Songs, sonnets and blank verse were traditional ways for a lover to express his love. The audience enjoys watching Benedick's lack of skill in singing and verse-making (lines 18–31), but which of his remarks most movingly expresses how love has moved his very soul?

Write Benedick's pitiful attempt at a love poem for Beatrice. Incorporate the legendary lovers, Hero and Leander, and Troilus and Cressida (see pp. 104 and 183). Use the rhymes Benedick mentions.

---

deserve . . . hands earn my gratitude
helping . . . speech of getting me a chance to talk to
comely fitting
keep . . . stairs remain a servant
catches seizes on (bawdy meanings)
I give . . . bucklers I surrender

panders go-betweens
quondam former
carpet-mongers frequenters of ladies' bedrooms
in festival terms in the style of public display (i.e. speaking poetry)

Act 5 Scene 2
Leonato's garden

Enter BENEDICK and MARGARET

BENEDICK Pray thee, sweet Mistress Margaret, deserve well at my
hands, by helping me to the speech of Beatrice.

MARGARET Will you then write me a sonnet in praise of my beauty?

BENEDICK In so high a style, Margaret, that no man living shall come
over it, for in most comely truth thou deservest it.   5

MARGARET To have no man come over me, why, shall I always keep
below stairs?

BENEDICK Thy wit is as quick as the greyhound's mouth, it catches.

MARGARET And yours, as blunt as the fencers' foils, which hit, but hurt
not.   10

BENEDICK A most manly wit, Margaret, it will not hurt a woman: and so
I pray thee call Beatrice, I give thee the bucklers.

MARGARET Give us the swords, we have bucklers of our own.

BENEDICK If you use them, Margaret, you must put in the pikes with a
vice, and they are dangerous weapons for maids.   15

MARGARET Well, I will call Beatrice to you, who I think hath legs. *Exit*

BENEDICK And therefore will come.

[*Sings*]   The God of love
                                      That sits above,
                                      And knows me,   20
                                      And knows me:
                                      How pitiful I deserve.

I mean in singing, but in loving – Leander the good swimmer,
Troilus, the first employer of panders, and a whole book full of
these quondam carpet-mongers, whose names yet run smoothly in   25
the even road of a blank verse, why they were never so truly turned
over and over as my poor self in love: marry, I cannot show it in
rhyme, I have tried: I can find out no rhyme to lady but baby, an
innocent rhyme: for scorn horn, a hard rhyme: for school fool, a
babbling rhyme: very ominous endings. No, I was not born under a   30
rhyming planet, nor I cannot woo in festival terms.

Benedick tells Beatrice that he has challenged Claudio and then asks her how she first fell in love with him. She in turn asks Benedick how he first fell in love with him.

---

1 Swords, shields or truth (in groups of four)

Even when they are genuinely courting, Benedick and Beatrice cannot stop arguing. 'Thou and I are too wise to woo peaceably', he remarks in line 54. Their 'merry war', however, has a new playfulness to it. In their opening exchange (lines 32–5), for example, Benedick asks her to 'stay but till then' (i.e. until he asks her to go), so she jokingly replies that since he has just said 'then', she had better be off!

Decide just how much their old hostilities have abated. Two of you sit face to face and slowly read lines 32–79. The other two sit beside each character and arm themselves with an imaginary sword and a book as a shield.

As Beatrice and Benedick speak, the other two must mime a sword thrust if they think their character is attacking, raise the shield if they are on the defensive and put both sword and shield down if they are being truly open, sympathetic and honest. Change roles and try it again.

Afterwards, compare the way Beatrice and Benedick talk to each other here with the way they spoke to each other in Act 1 Scene 1 and Act 2 Scene 1. It is also helpful to contrast their way of courting with Hero and Claudio's (for example, look back at the latter's betrothal in Act 2 Scene 1, lines 225–40).

2 'Thou' and 'you' again

Which pronoun form does Benedick use to address Beatrice and how does she address him? Can you explain the difference? (Page 166 may help you.) Keep a note of how they address each other from now on.

---

that I came   what I came for (i.e. to know about the challenge)
noisome   disgusting, smelly
undergoes   accepts
subscribe him   write him down as
so politic a state   such a well-organised rule

suffer   (1) experience (2) put up with
spite it   trouble it
there's not . . . himself   self-praise is no recommendation
instance   saying, proverb
that . . . neighbours   untrue now

Enter BEATRICE

Sweet Beatrice, wouldst thou come when I called thee?

BEATRICE Yea, signor, and depart when you bid me.

BENEDICK Oh stay but till then.

BEATRICE Then, is spoken: fare you well now, and yet ere I go, let me 35
go with that I came, which is, with knowing what hath passed
between you and Claudio.

BENEDICK Only foul words, and thereupon I will kiss thee.

BEATRICE Foul words is but foul wind, and foul wind is but foul breath,
and foul breath is noisome, therefore I will depart unkissed. 40

BENEDICK Thou hast frighted the word out of his right sense, so forc-
ible is thy wit: but I must tell thee plainly, Claudio undergoes my
challenge, and either I must shortly hear from him, or I will subscribe him a coward: and I pray thee now tell me, for which of my
bad parts didst thou first fall in love with me? 45

BEATRICE For them all together, which maintained so politic a state of
evil, that they will not admit any good part to intermingle with them:
but for which of my good parts did you first suffer love for me?

BENEDICK Suffer love! A good epithet: I do suffer love indeed, for I
love thee against my will. 50

BEATRICE In spite of your heart I think: alas poor heart, if you spite it
for my sake, I will spite it for yours, for I will never love that which
my friend hates.

BENEDICK Thou and I are too wise to woo peaceably.

BEATRICE It appears not in this confession, there's not one wise man 55
among twenty that will praise himself.

BENEDICK An old, an old instance, Beatrice, that lived in the time of
good neighbours: if a man do not erect in this age his own tomb ere
he dies, he shall live no longer in monument than the bell rings and
the widow weeps. 60

As Benedick and Beatrice talk, Ursula comes rushing in with news that Don John's plot has been discovered and Hero's good name restored. All three leave in haste for Leonato's house.

'Coming to a mutual likeness.' Look at the pictures of Beatrice and Benedick in the colour picture section and on pp. 32, 118, 126, 169, 175, 177 and 194. Talk together about their changing moods and attitudes through the play. How would you describe their relationship in this scene?

Question   Good question!
clamour   noise (of the funeral bell)
rheum   weeping (of the widow)
Don Worm   in the Bible, conscience is a tormenting worm eating a man's spirit
be the trumpet . . . virtues   blow his own trumpet

mend   get better
yonder's old coil   there's an awful commotion
abused   deceived, imposed upon
presently   immediately
die in thy lap   (sexual innuendo)

BEATRICE And how long is that think you?

BENEDICK Question: why an hour in clamour and a quarter in rheum, therefore is it most expedient for the wise, if Don Worm (his conscience) find no impediment to the contrary, to be the trumpet of his own virtues, as I am to myself; so much for praising myself, who I myself will bear witness is praiseworthy: and now tell me, how doth your cousin?　　65

BEATRICE Very ill.

BENEDICK And how do you?

BEATRICE Very ill too.　　70

BENEDICK Serve God, love me, and mend: there will I leave you too, for here comes one in haste.

Enter URSULA

URSULA Madam you must come to your uncle, yonder's old coil at home, it is proved my Lady Hero hath been falsely accused, the prince and Claudio mightily abused, and Don John is the author of all, who is fled and gone: will you come presently?　　75

BEATRICE Will you go hear this news, signor?

BENEDICK I will live in thy heart, die in thy lap, and be buried in thy eyes: and moreover, I will go with thee to thy uncle's.

Exeunt

Night. In a sombre ceremony, Claudio fulfils the first part of his promise. A tribute to Hero is read out, a solemn hymn is sung and a vow made to commemorate the anniversary of her death.

---

1 A grim reminder (in groups of about seven)

In Act 4 the play moved from light into dark. Now it moves back from darkness into light, both literally (lines 24–8) and symbolically. At the start of Scene 3 in one production, the lights dimmed, a tomb-like monument rose up from beneath the stage, and shadowy figures entered bearing flickering torches.

The best thing to do with Scene 3 is to act it out. Take parts and create your own dramatically effective scene of solemn ritual. Consider:

- using choral speaking and echo effects
- highlighting the sound patterns of the rhymed verse
- the stage direction 'Enter . . . with tapers and music'.

2 Who says what?

No one can be quite sure about who Shakespeare intended to speak lines 3–23. One production had:

- Claudio speaking the epitaph (lines 3–10) and lines 22–3
- Balthasar singing the song (lines 12–21).

How would you allocate the lines? Give reasons for your choices.

3 Did Claudio write the epitaph? (in groups of three)

In Act 5 Scene 1, Leonato instructed Claudio to compose an epitaph to hang on Hero's tomb. Read the actual epitaph (lines 3–10) and debate whether it sounds like the sort of thing Claudio would write.

---

tapers   lighted candles
monument   tomb, burial chamber
guerdon of   recompense for
ith shame   of shame
ddess of the night   Diana, moon
  dess and patroness of virgins

virgin knight   devout servant (Hero, a virgin, is imagined as a follower of Diana)
Till death be utterèd   until our grief has been fully expressed
rite   ceremony

Act 5 Scene 3
Hero's monument

Enter CLAUDIO, DON PEDRO and three or four Attendants with tapers
and music

CLAUDIO Is this the monument of Leonato?
LORD It is, my lord.

> [*He reads the*] *epitaph*
> Done to death by slanderous tongues,
> Was the Hero that here lies:
> Death in guerdon of her wrongs,   5
> Gives her fame which never dies:
> So the life that died with shame,
> Lives in death with glorious fame.
> Hang thou there upon the tomb,
> Praising her when I am dumb.   10

CLAUDIO Now music sound and sing your solemn hymn.

> *Song*
> Pardon, goddess of the night,
> Those that slew thy virgin knight,
> For the which with songs of woe,
> Round about her tomb they go: 15
> Midnight assist our moan,
> Help us to sigh and groan.
> Heavily, heavily.
> Graves yawn and yield your dead,
> Till death be utterèd,   20
> Heavily, heavily.

LORD
> Now unto thy bones good night,
> Yearly will I do this rite.

As dawn breaks, Don Pedro and Claudio leave to dress suitably for the marriage. Scene 4 opens with Leonato sending the women to mask themselves in readiness for the ceremony.

---

1 A ghostly Hero

In the 1996 RSC production, a door opened in the monument to reveal a ghost-image of the 'dead' Hero. Find the two verse lines Claudio speaks in Act 5 Scene 1 which might have suggested this staging.

2 Night ends and a new day begins

Dawn seems to be breaking at the end of Scene 3, after a troubled and sombre night. You are about to read the final scene. Before you do, guess what will happen to the major characters. See if your predictions come true.

Phoebus Apollo, the sun god, who drives his chariot across the sky
several separate
weeds clothes (What does this change of clothes symbolise?)
Hymen god of marriage
issue outcome

Than this Hero's death
Upon the error as a result of the error
question investigation
sorts have turned out
confirmed countenance a straight face

DON PEDRO Good morrow, masters, put your torches out,
        The wolves have preyed, and look, the gentle day   25
        Before the wheels of Phoebus, round about
        Dapples the drowsy east with spots of grey:
        Thanks to you all, and leave us, fare you well.
CLAUDIO Good morrow, masters, each his several way.

                        [Exeunt Attendants]

DON PEDRO Come let us hence, and put on other weeds,   30
        And then to Leonato's we will go.
CLAUDIO And Hymen now with luckier issue speeds,
        Than this for whom we rendered up this woe.

                                Exeunt

Act 5   Scene 4
Leonato's house

Enter LEONATO, BENEDICK, MARGARET, URSULA, ANTONIO,
                FRIAR FRANCIS and HERO

FRIAR FRANCIS Did I not tell you she was innocent?
LEONATO So are the prince and Claudio who accused her,
        Upon the error that you heard debated:
        But Margaret was in some fault for this,
        Although against her will as it appears,   5
        In the true course of all the question.
ANTONIO Well, I am glad that all things sorts so well.
BENEDICK And so am I, being else by faith enforced
        To call young Claudio to a reckoning for it.
LEONATO Well, daughter, and you gentlewomen all,   10
        Withdraw into a chamber by yourselves,
        And when I send for you come hither masked:
        The prince and Claudio promised by this hour
        To visit me: you know your office, brother,
        You must be father to your brother's daughter,   15
        And give her to young Claudio.

                            Exeunt Ladies

ANTONIO Which I will do with confirmed countenance.

Benedick requests Beatrice's hand in marriage, to which Leonato willingly agrees. Claudio and Don Pedro arrive for the wedding ceremony and continue their mockery of the lovestruck Benedick.

---

1 'Your answer, sir, is enigmatical' (in pairs)

Benedick formally asks permission to marry Beatrice (lines 21–31) and seems confused by Leonato's 'enigmatical' (puzzling) responses. Read lines 21–31 to each other. Do you think Benedick is still unaware of the trick played on him?

2 Good friends once again? (in groups of three)

When Benedick, Claudio and Don Pedro last met (Act 5 Scene 1, lines 109–73), relations between them were strained. Benedick challenged Claudio and there was considerable hostility.

Sit face to face and read lines 40–52 (up to 'I owe you'). Is your mockery friendly or aggressive? Are you all friends again? The 'thou/you' pronouns may give you some ideas (see p. 166). So, too, may the vivid image of a 'February face' that Don Pedro uses to describe Benedick's expression (lines 41–2).

3 Mighty Jove and the beautiful Europa

Jupiter (Jove), king of the gods, took on the form of a bull in order to carry off Europa, the beautiful daughter of a Phoenician king (see p. 183). Europa also means Europe.

Which of Benedick's comments in Act 1 Scene 1 is Claudio hinting at in lines 43–7? Explain how Benedick's reply turns the insult back onto Claudio.

---

intreat ... pains   beg to trouble you
undo   ruin
lent her   encouraged her to have
requite her   return her love
sight whereof   way of seeing which
will   desire
my will is, ...   my will is that ...

hold my mind   keep to my intention
Ethiop   black (pale skin was a mark of beauty – see p. 187)
tip thy horns with gold   make you look a fine cuckold
low   bellow
got   fathered

BENEDICK Friar, I must intreat your pains, I think.

FRIAR FRANCIS To do what, signor?

BENEDICK To bind me, or undo me, one of them: 20
        Signor Leonato, truth it is, good signor,
        Your niece regards me with an eye of favour.

LEONATO That eye my daughter lent her, 'tis most true.

BENEDICK And I do with an eye of love requite her.

LEONATO The sight whereof I think you had from me,   25
        From Claudio and the prince, but what's your will?

BENEDICK Your answer, sir, is enigmatical,
        But for my will, my will is, your good will
        May stand with ours, this day to be conjoined,
        In the state of honourable marriage,   30
        In which (good friar) I shall desire your help.

LEONATO My heart is with your liking.

FRIAR FRANCIS   And my help.
        Here comes the prince and Claudio.

Enter DON PEDRO *and* CLAUDIO, *with Attendants*

DON PEDRO Good morrow to this fair assembly.

LEONATO Good morrow, prince, good morrow, Claudio: 35
        We here attend you, are you yet determined,
        Today to marry with my brother's daughter?

CLAUDIO I'll hold my mind were she an Ethiop.

LEONATO Call her forth, brother, here's the friar ready.
                             [*Exit Antonio*]

DON PEDRO Good morrow, Benedick, why what's the matter,   40
        That you have such a February face,
        So full of frost, of storm, and cloudiness?

CLAUDIO I think he thinks upon the savage bull:
        Tush fear not, man, we'll tip thy horns with gold,
        And all Europa shall rejoice at thee,   45
        As once Europa did at lusty Jove,
        When he would play the noble beast in love.

BENEDICK Bull Jove, sir, had an amiable low,
        And some such strange bull leaped your father's cow,
        And got a calf in that same noble feat,   50
        Much like to you, for you have just his bleat.

Antonio brings in four masked ladies. Claudio accepts his unknown bride and discovers she is Hero. Beatrice and Benedick realise they have been tricked into believing that each was in love with the other.

1 Masking and unmasking (in groups of seven)

This is a serious and tense moment for Claudio and Hero. Because all the women who enter are in disguise, Claudio has no idea who is to be his bride and Hero will be awaiting his reaction when she unmasks. Beatrice and Benedick, for their part, will be required to remove their psychological masks and publicly admit their love. Choose from the following:

a Act out lines 52–71. Make this strange second betrothal a solemn and moving occasion (see picture on p. 163). Use masks or veils, and think about the timing of the actual moment of unmasking. At the end of your dramatisation, Claudio and Hero should speak in role explaining their actions.

b Shakespeare used this unmasking device to powerful dramatic effect in other plays. In *The Winter's Tale*, for example, a 'dead' wife is found to be alive (she too had been wronged and kept hidden just as Hero has been). Talk together about the meaning of this strange unmasking ceremony. Why must there be a 'new' Hero? Do we also have a 'new' Claudio?

c 'No more than reason' (lines 74 and 77). Explore different ways of saying these lines. What do you think Beatrice and Benedick mean?

d Rehearse your version of lines 72–96. After the solemnity of Claudio and Hero's betrothal, make this event more light-hearted. Some Benedicks have gone up and down the line of masked ladies trying to find Beatrice (line 72). One Beatrice kept changing places to avoid being discovered. Many productions also get laughs from the business with the sonnets, and again with the kiss at line 96.

For this I owe you I'll pay you back
 for this
reckonings obligations
defiled slandered
but whiles only so long as
qualify moderate

largely in full, in detail
let wonder seem familiar treat your
 amazement as an everyday event
Soft and fair wait a minute
but in . . . recompense only as a
 friend

Enter ANTONIO, HERO, BEATRICE, MARGARET [*and*]
URSULA [*masked*]

CLAUDIO For this I owe you: here comes other reckonings.
　　　　 Which is the lady I must seize upon?
LEONATO This same is she, and I do give you her.
CLAUDIO Why then she's mine, sweet, let me see your face.　　　　55
LEONATO No that you shall not, till you take her hand,
　　　　 Before this friar, and swear to marry her.
CLAUDIO Give me your hand before this holy friar,
　　　　 I am your husband if you like of me.
HERO And when I lived I was your other wife,　　　　　　　　60
　　　　 And when you loved, you were my other husband.
CLAUDIO Another Hero?
HERO　　　　　　　　　　　Nothing certainer.
　　　　 One Hero died defiled, but I do live,
　　　　 And surely as I live, I am a maid.
DON PEDRO The former Hero, Hero that is dead.　　　　　　65
LEONATO She died, my lord, but whiles her slander lived.
FRIAR FRANCIS All this amazement can I qualify,
　　　　 When after that the holy rites are ended,
　　　　 I'll tell you largely of fair Hero's death:
　　　　 Meantime let wonder seem familiar,　　　　　　　　70
　　　　 And to the chapel let us presently.
BENEDICK Soft and fair friar, which is Beatrice?
BEATRICE I answer to that name, what is your will?
BENEDICK Do not you love me?
BEATRICE　　　　　　　　　　Why no, no more than reason.
BENEDICK Why then your uncle, and the prince, and Claudio,　75
　　　　 Have been deceived, they swore you did.
BEATRICE Do not you love me?
BENEDICK　　　　　　　　　　Troth no, no more than reason.
BEATRICE Why then my cousin, Margaret and Ursula
　　　　 Are much deceived, for they did swear you did.
BENEDICK They swore that you were almost sick for me.　　80
BEATRICE They swore that you were wellnigh dead for me.
BENEDICK 'Tis no such matter, then you do not love me?
BEATRICE No truly, but in friendly recompense.
LEONATO Come, cousin, I am sure you love the gentleman.
CLAUDIO And I'll be sworn upon't, that he loves her,　　　　85

159

After being confronted with the love sonnets they have both written, Beatrice and Benedick agree to accept each other. Benedick and Claudio are reconciled. News comes of Don John's capture. The dancing begins.

1 Ending the play (in small groups)

It is the convention in a comedy that all differences are eventually resolved. But how happy should the play's final moments be? Explore your views on the play's ending through one or more of the following:

a Benedick dominates the final moments of the play, but why is Beatrice so uncharacteristically silent? Write her thoughts.

b Act out a version of lines 104–12 in which Hero and Beatrice play a part in reconciling Claudio and Benedick. Then try a more hostile final encounter between the two men.

c Talk together about the kind of music and dancing that would most fittingly end the play. Think back to the masked dance in Act 2 Scene 1 and decide how different you would want this final dance to be.

d Don Pedro is often left to stand alone at the end of the play. What are his thoughts as he watches the dancers?

e Look back in the colour picture section at one production's final moments (p. xii, bottom). Devise the closing image (the last thing the audience sees as the lights dim) for a production by each of the following: a feminist director (focusing upon power in male–female relationships), a Marxist director (money and power are dominant), a Freudian director (unconscious desires dominate). Then devise the closing image for your own production.

f Organise the curtain call and decide on a typical gesture/action for each character. Who enters and leaves with whom?

---

consumption   a deadly wasting disease
witcrackers   jokers
flout   mock
care for   am hurt by
epigram   short witty poem
a shall wear   he shall wear

double dealer   (1) married man (2) deceiver (i.e. unfaithful husband)
do not . . . narrowly to thee   does not keep a very close eye on you
staff . . . horn   staff of office or walking stick (with cuckolding hints, of course)
ta'en   captured

　　　　　For here's a paper written in his hand,
　　　　　A halting sonnet of his own pure brain,
　　　　　Fashioned to Beatrice.
HERO　　　　　　　　　　　　　And here's another,
　　　　　Writ in my cousin's hand, stol'n from her pocket,
　　　　　Containing her affection unto Benedick.　　　　　　　　90

BENEDICK A miracle, here's our own hands against our hearts: come, I
　　　　will have thee, but by this light I take thee for pity.

BEATRICE I would not deny you, but by this good day, I yield upon great
　　　　persuasion, and partly to save your life, for I was told, you were in a
　　　　consumption.　　　　　　　　　　　　　　　　　　　95

BENEDICK Peace I will stop your mouth.

DON PEDRO How dost thou, Benedick the married man?

BENEDICK I'll tell thee what, prince: a college of witcrackers cannot
　　　　flout me out of my humour: dost thou think I care for a satire or an
　　　　epigram? No, if a man will be beaten with brains, a shall wear　　100
　　　　nothing handsome about him: in brief, since I do purpose to marry,
　　　　I will think nothing to any purpose that the world can say against it,
　　　　and therefore never flout at me, for what I have said against it: for
　　　　man is a giddy thing, and this is my conclusion: for thy part,
　　　　Claudio, I did think to have beaten thee, but in that thou art like to　　105
　　　　be my kinsman, live unbruised, and love my cousin.

CLAUDIO I had well hoped thou wouldst have denied Beatrice, that I
　　　　might have cudgelled thee out of thy single life, to make thee a
　　　　double dealer, which out of question thou wilt be, if my cousin do
　　　　not look exceeding narrowly to thee.　　　　　　　　110

BENEDICK Come, come, we are friends, let's have a dance ere we are
　　　　married, that we may lighten our own hearts, and our wives' heels.

LEONATO We'll have dancing afterward.

BENEDICK First, of my word, therefore play music. Prince, thou art sad,
　　　　get thee a wife, get thee a wife, there is no staff more reverend than　　115
　　　　one tipped with horn.

Enter MESSENGER

MESSENGER My lord, your brother John is ta'en in flight,
　　　　And brought with armed men back to Messina.

BENEDICK Think not on him till tomorrow, I'll devise thee brave
　　　　punishments for him: strike up, pipers.　　　　　　　　120
　　　　　　　　　Dance [and exeunt]

Looking back at the play
Activities for groups or individuals

Mini-saga

A 'mini-saga challenge' requires you to tell a story in exactly fifty words. Write the events of Act 5 as a mini-saga. Read your version and listen to other people's mini-sagas. What are the key events that you have all included?

Moods

Act 5 contains many changes of mood: grief, despair, anger, vengeance, repentance, love, mockery, celebration. Prepare director's notes for Act 5. Indicate when and where you want to create a change of mood (on which entrances and which lines).

Then act out your 'Mood change show'. You might call out the mood and have a character deliver the relevant lines in an appropriate tone. You could use mime, or a combination of words, actions and pictures.

Cliffhangers

Imagine that the story of *Much Ado About Nothing* is to be dramatised in a new six-part television series. Divide the play into six parts and perform the last minute of each episode. Remember that you must end episodes one to five on a note of suspense so that your audience will watch the following week.

A penitent Claudio and a reborn Hero

For a modern audience Claudio's seemingly light 'punishment' for such a cruel shaming of Hero is not easy to take: public admission of her innocence, one night's vigil and she is offered to him a second time.

a Look back at what Claudio says and how he behaves in Act 5. One person collects evidence to show he is genuinely penitent. The other collects evidence to show he is shallow and insincere. Join together to debate the question.

b At the abortive wedding, the Friar hoped that from the 'travail' (suffering) would come a 'greater birth' (Act 4 Scene 1, line 206).

Some see Claudio's mourning vigil and Hero's second betrothal as a kind of ritualistic death and rebirth. Claudio's acceptance of his masked bride demonstrates the truth of his love for the 'dead' Hero, while Hero unmasks to reveal the truth of her chastity.

Look back at the episode where Antonio brings in his 'niece' with three other masked ladies (Act 5 Scene 4, lines 52–71). Talk about how a production might make the creation of a 'new' Claudio and a 'new' Hero dramatically credible.

Claudio and Hero's second 'masked' betrothal.

Is the future bright for Beatrice and Benedick?

Could such a free spirit as Beatrice ever endure playing the role of the obedient Elizabethan wife, 'Taming [her] wild heart' to Benedick's 'loving hand' (Act 3 Scene 1, line 112)?

It is five years later. The couple are visitors at Leonato's house, together with Claudio and Hero. Which of the two couples is more secure and happy? Are Benedick and Claudio fully reconciled? To explore these issues choose one of the following:

a Improvise this reunion scene, then write a script for it.

b Improvise what happens when the two couples go to see a marriage guidance counsellor. Afterwards, write the script of the meeting to become part of a TV documentary.

c Interview the couples as a reporter for a popular weekly magazine. Write the article.

What is the play about?

Much ado about many things

Much Ado About Nothing has always been a popular play. A verse published in 1640 showed how it filled theatres:

> Let but Beatrice
> And Benedick be seen, lo in a trice
> The Cockpit, galleries, boxes, all are full.

The appeal of the 'merry war' has a lot to do with the play's lasting popularity, but there are many more reasons. Its themes have universal appeal: love, status, relationships between men and women, the ways in which we perceive one another. The moods of the play swing from light comedy to dark, life-endangering menace. There is always something happening: a fresh break-out of an old conflict, another plot, another mistaking, even songs and dancing!

- ◆ List four themes you think Shakespeare is exploring in the play. Alongside each, write a sentence saying how the theme is still relevant today.
- ◆ A modern English version of *Much Ado About Nothing* is about to go on peak-time popular television. Write a script for a two-minute trailer for this programme. Your trailer will give the audience ten reasons for watching.

Two pairs of lovers

The Beatrice–Benedick story seems to be Shakespeare's own invention, but the Hero–Claudio narrative has a long history. The tale of how a lover is deceived into believing that his beloved has been unfaithful to him because he has seen a man at her bedroom window goes back many centuries. Shakespeare probably based his Hero–Claudio story on Italian versions popular in Elizabethan England.

- ◆ Step into role as Shakespeare. Write his letter home to his wife telling her why he is pairing a 'modern' love story with a 'traditional' one.
- ◆ Write an assignment which identifies incidents in contemporary plays and television programmes which draw on the Hero–Claudio story.

Reflecting Elizabethan society and everyday life

Despite the foreign names, Messina is a very English community, much like the household of a wealthy Elizabethan lord. Many Elizabethan sports and pastimes are mentioned in the play: angling, archery, falconry, eating and drinking, gambling, brothel-haunting, fighting.

◆ Assign each scene in the play to a particular place and time of day. Include in your time/place pattern all of the domestic events and ceremonies that take place in this community (e.g. meals, weddings, funerals).

Many prosperous Elizabethan merchants and landowners sought to climb up into the ranks of the aristocracy, rather as Leonato's family does. This tension between the old aristocratic order and the newly wealthy commercial class is very much reflected in the play. Leonato at first shows suitable respect for his noble guests. He is clearly delighted to have Count Claudio as a future son-in-law and he believes the accusations made against Hero simply because his superiors said so (Act 4 Scene 1, line 145). At first only Beatrice and the Friar believe Hero's story. But their conviction wins over first Benedick, then Leonato and Antonio, until all three in turn challenge Claudio in the most insulting manner (Act 5 Scene 1, lines 45–173).

◆ Pool your ideas and write down your impressions of the society Shakespeare shows us. Think in particular of the treatment of Hero and the 'penance' Claudio is made to suffer for his unforgivable behaviour.

Male power, status and honour

Men and male values dominated Elizabethan society. Every Elizabethan male was expected to train to fight for his country if needed. Sunday practice with the longbow at the archery butts was obligatory (Act 2 Scene 1, lines 186–7). Close bonds of male friendship, especially ones forged in war, were very much valued, but a man prized his honour and reputation above all else.

◆ Don Pedro and Claudio are described by Benedick as absolutely honourable (Act 4 Scene 1, line 179). Write a sentence/paragraph giving your opinion of their 'honourable' qualities.

'Thou/thee/thine' and 'you/your'

Use of these pronouns and adjectives sent very clear social signals in Shakespeare's time. When addressing one person, the use of 'you' implied distance, suggesting respect for your superior, or courtesy to your social equal. 'Thou' could imply either closeness or superiority. It could signal friendship towards an equal or superiority over a servant. Used to address one of higher rank, it was aggressive and insulting.

◆ Rank, respect, allegiance and friendship are put to the test when Claudio denounces Hero. Identify how Benedick and Leonato use the 'thou/you' forms in Act 5 to address Claudio.
◆ Explore how Benedick's growing love for Beatrice changes the way he addresses her in Acts 4 and 5. Can you explain why Beatrice still keeps to the 'you' form to address him, even in the final scenes?
◆ Explain why Dogberry uses both 'thou' and 'you' to address Borachio and Conrade in Act 4 Scene 2.
◆ The people of rank in the play are all men. Don Pedro and his brother are princes, Claudio is a count (equivalent to an English earl), while 'signors' Benedick and Leonato are gentlemen of lower rank. When these men address each other in Act 1, do they speak strictly according to their status?

Tangled webs (in small groups)

The play has three major dramatic plots or stories. The main plot is the Hero–Claudio love story, while the 'gulling' of Beatrice and Benedick and Don John's ruining of Hero's reputation are the two sub-plots. The close-knit nature of Messina society, where everybody wants to know everybody else's business, is reflected in the way in which these three plots are so closely interwoven.

On a large piece of paper, make three columns for the three plots and write the scenes in order down the left-hand side. On this grid briefly record, scene by scene, each stage in the development of each plot and the names of the characters involved in the action. Work as a group to share the workload.

◆ Which characters are most entangled in the events of all three plots?
◆ Which characters are the catalysts or the initiators of events?
◆ The Hero–Claudio story is technically the main plot because it sparks off all other events in the play. Write a paragraph showing how what happens in the Beatrice–Benedick and Don John sub-plots results from Claudio's love for Hero.

Tricks, hoaxes and deceptions

The play contains many tricks and deceptions, both deliberate and accidental.

◆ Malevolent and benevolent plots, deliberate and accidental deceptions. Compile your own collection of each.
◆ One writer said that the play 'is composed of three hoaxes, four withheld secrets and three metamorphoses' (a 'metamorphosis' is a profound change). Identify what each of these might be, and use your findings to write an extended essay titled: 'Hoaxes, secrets and profound changes in *Much Ado About Nothing*'.

Nothing and noting, truth and illusion

The punning on 'nothing' and 'noting' in the title (see pp. 10 and 50) suggests from the start that the play will be concerned with ways in which people perceive one another. Characters are continually faced with the question 'Can I be certain that what I see, or hear or know, is true?' Their difficulties are often caused by the deliberate deceptions of others, but equally often stem from self-deception or their own human fallibility.

◆ 'Men were deceivers ever'. Kenneth Branagh's 1993 film of *Much Ado About Nothing* begins with Beatrice ironically speaking the song (from Act 2 Scene 3) 'Sigh no more, ladies, sigh no more'. Turn to page 53 to remind yourself of the song. Then talk together about how much you think it catches the spirit of the whole play.
◆ *Deliberate deception, self-deception* and *human fallibility*. Make a list of the problems facing characters in the play under these three headings. Use your list to write about the ways in which you think the play explores a problem that we all face: 'How can I ever know the truth for certain?'
◆ The Truth and Illusion Theatre Company have come to Messina to present a show which will reveal all the deceptions and self-deceptions that have taken place during the past few days. Be as inventive as you can in presenting a short drama that highlights the play's many comic and serious deceptions.

Women in a patriarchal world

Men (particularly fathers) dominated Elizabethan society. Traditional assumptions of male superiority were widespread. A wife should submit to her husband. She was his legal property and was rarely expected to think for herself.

However, women in London enjoyed a greater degree of freedom. Queen Elizabeth I showed that a woman could match any man. She was highly educated, fluent in several languages and a skilful politician.

Elizabethan men drew on a variety of stereotyped views about women as they attempted to explain, justify and control the subordinate place of woman in society:

Woman as whore or wife   Women had just two functions. They were either prostitutes to be bought or wives to be owned.

Woman as goddess   The courtly lover placed women on a pedestal. But is to worship a woman as a goddess to silence her as a human being?

Woman as adulterer   Virginity was a virtue and female adultery an unforgivable sin. An heiress proved unchaste was deprived of her inheritance.

Woman as shrew and scapegoat   Women were often blamed by men for all the faults of the world. A woman who spoke up for herself was a 'curst' shrew and needed taming.

◆ *Much Ado About Nothing* explores (and challenges) a wide range of men's attitudes to the place of women in society. Use the information above to make a list of comments made by men in the play which echo these attitudes. Also note down quotations where even women express similar sentiments.

◆ In a world of men, the women of Messina have two main options: to submit or to resist. Hero submits. Wooed first by the prince, then given to Claudio and promptly rejected, she is given a second time to the very man who had so cruelly spurned her.

  – Write a script in which a director and the actor playing Hero discuss how to give credibility to Hero's silence and compliance.

  – Beatrice clearly resists. Start with her interruption of the Messenger in Act 1 Scene 1, and list the times when she shows her independence and defiance. Use your findings to write a character study of Beatrice (pp. 174–5 may help you).

Finding love in the world of Messina

Claudio and Hero's story demonstrates the conventional rituals of aristocratic Elizabethan courtship and marriage: wooing by proxy, settlement of the dowry, formal betrothal, wedding ceremony. To these Shakespeare adds a second 'masked betrothal' which resolves the story.

◆ Write down these five stages and next to each speculate on the nature of Claudio and Hero's feelings for each other at that moment. Give evidence from the play where possible and your reasons for thinking whether they find true love or not.

◆ Although Beatrice and Benedick's journey from hostility to love is long and difficult, many commentators think that their story culminates in a 'marriage of true minds', a union of equals. But will they 'live happily ever after'? Write several paragraphs giving your views on whether Beatrice and Benedick's final kiss symbolises the love and harmony that they have learned to share, or demonstrates that the voluble lady has finally had her mouth stopped.

This is how the 1968 Royal Shakespeare Company production showed the moment when Beatrice and Benedick found love. How would *you* stage this moment?

Fashion and appearance

The Elizabethan aristocrat was a rich and glittering sight. Costumes for both sexes were extremely ornate and vastly expensive. The way you dressed was an indication of your rank and people were forbidden by law from wearing fabrics belonging to higher ranks. For example, Cloth of Gold, a material woven with pure gold threads (see Act 3 Scene 4, lines 14–18), could only be worn by royalty and nobility.

Men's fashions

In the eyes of the traditionalists, men's fashions had become particularly effeminate by the end of the sixteenth century. Some noblemen wore make-up, had their hair curled at the barber's, smothered themselves in perfume, and wore single earrings and lovelocks (see picture opposite). This last fashion particularly angered the moralists of the day.

The fashionable English gallant also copied any foreign style that took his fancy. Such extremes in dress meant that the Englishman was often laughed at for his outrageous mixing of foreign fashions (see Act 3 Scene 2, lines 24–30). The stylish combination for 1599 was German or Dutch trunk hose, French doublet, Spanish hat and Italian neckwear. Foreigners often commented on how frequently the English changed their fashions, particularly their hats, which 'ever changed with the next block' (Act 1 Scene 1, line 56). A 'block' was the wooden mould used to help form a hat into the desired shape.

Such lavish ostentation made some Elizabethans very uneasy. They thought the aristocracy should be investing in their estates and not spending their wealth on clothes. Huge debts were accumulated as the nobility kept striving to outdo, or outdress, each other.

The fashionable aristocrat of 1599 (could this be Count Claudio?)

The Earl of Southampton (see portrait on p. 171) was Shakespeare's patron. Shakespeare dedicated two long poems to him: *Venus and Adonis* and *The Rape of Lucrece*. Many believe that he may be the young man to whom Shakespeare addressed many of his sonnets.

This portrait of the Earl of Southampton, painted at about the time the play was written, shows him dressed in the latest style. His doublet has very little padding (the heavily padded peascod doublet was beginning to go out of fashion) but his trunk hose are still very heavily padded.

Notice the expensive gloves, the ornate armour and the long lovelock trailing over his left shoulder.

'What a deformed thief this fashion is'

Costumes for both sexes distorted the natural human shape. The fashionable male peascod doublet was heavily padded in front to give the appearance of a large paunch. The male trunk hose (breeches) were also padded to accentuate this pear shape. Women's costumes were even more extreme and uncomfortable (see p. 88). Corsets formed tiny waists and stomachers flattened the breasts and abdomen. Clumsy metal farthingales ballooned the skirts into a huge bell shape.

Much ado about appearance?

a Fashion words and pictures fill the play. List all the fashion/ appearance words you can find in the opening scene.

b From the information on pages 84, 88 and 170–2, write several sentences giving your view on whether Borachio was right to comment so cynically on Elizabethan fashion in Act 3 Scene 3.

c Read Act 3 Scene 2, lines 1–54 and decide how much like a fashionable Elizabethan gallant Benedick has become. Suggest how the actor (and the other characters on stage) could highlight the changes.

d The Watch, being lower-class, would wear very different clothes from the aristocrats. Design their costumes for an Elizabethan, Victorian or modern-day production (see examples in the colour picture section and on pp. 80, 180 and 193).

e Choose a character each and identify the fashion words/images he or she uses during the course of the play.

f Find lines or words about fashion which help to convey the difficulty of knowing the difference between outward show and inner truth.

g Where in the play do dress and costume take on a serious and symbolic significance?

Kenneth Branagh said about his 1993 film of *Much Ado About Nothing* (see both pictures on p. vi in the colour section and the top picture on p. xii): 'We consciously avoided setting this version in a specific time, but instead went for a look and an atmosphere that worked within itself, where clothes, props, architecture, language and customs all belong to the same timeless world. This imaginary world could exist anywhere along a continuum from 1700 to 1900.'

Try your hand at designing a costume for either Beatrice or Benedick that has a 'timeless' quality.

A portrait of Mary Fitton, maid of honour to Queen Elizabeth I, in all the splendour of the richest of Elizabethan costumes. Search the library and the Internet for other examples of dress in Shakespeare's time. Use your findings, together with the information in this section and on pages 84, 88 and 140, to compile an assignment that presents evidence on the importance of fashion and appearance in the play.

Characters

Beatrice and Benedick: two scorners of love

Beatrice Actors must 'find' their character as the play comes to life around them in rehearsal and performance. Susan Fleetwood (see pp. 118 and 150) talks below about what she 'found' when she played Beatrice.

> Beatrice is life-giving, energetic, witty, intelligent, fun-loving, but lonely. In playing her, I was conscious of her as the orphaned cousin, being on the outside of things in many ways. Yet her position in the household also allows her freedom to be outrageous in a way that Hero cannot be.
>
> Beatrice has an absolute hatred of the hypocrisy of the age, of all the sham nonsense and social hierarchy which aims to control. She has no patience with all the military hyperbole and bravado and is also detached from all the courtly ceremony and ritual. That's why I stood apart from the group, waiting, observing, flexing the sword I'd just used in the mock fight with Leonato [see pp. 2 and 6].
>
> Beatrice doesn't only challenge the accepted opinion of war, she is critical of all masculine values. She is a mature woman who rages against the masculine solidarity which can so easily destroy a woman's reputation. She means it when she says 'Kill Claudio'.
>
> The choice that Benedick makes when Beatrice asks him to kill Claudio is critical to her entire future. Had he chosen otherwise, Beatrice might have been doomed to a future as an isolated, shrewish woman and Benedick to a future as a drunken roué [debaucher].
>
> At the end of the play Beatrice is a liberated character who flings herself into the dance in celebration. The kiss is a real physical commitment, indicative of her love and passion. Unless the audience really believes that Beatrice and Benedick want to be together, there is no real joy at the end.

Sinead Cusack (above opposite) was a young, self-confident, flirtatious Beatrice who really discomforted Benedick, until Hero's public shaming reduced her to impotent tears (see page 126).

Judi Dench (below opposite) played a Beatrice heading towards middle age. Central to her role was the reference to a previous encounter when Benedick had won her heart 'with false dice' (Act 2 Scene 1, lines 211–16) – a past betrayal which clearly still hurt her.

'When she says . . . "I would eat his heart in the market place"', wrote one reviewer of this Beatrice, 'you'd better believe it.'

'Thou and I are too wise to woo peaceably.' A more melancholy, 'smiling through sadness' Beatrice.

◆ **'Oh God that I were a man!'** Write an essay in which you describe the qualities you would hope to see in an ideal portrayal of Beatrice. Look at the performance history of *Much Ado About Nothing* (pp. 190–4) and use some of the activities on page 181 to help you clarify your ideas.

175

Benedick   From the start Benedick talks as if he were the eternal bachelor-soldier, a 'professed tyrant' to women (Act 1 Scene 1, lines 122–4), but it is clearly a pose, as he himself almost admits. Some Benedicks have swaggered initially, as if they were 'the life and soul of the party'; others have used their wit almost like a mask to hide a secret fear of women.

In many productions, Benedick finds himself bested in the word battles with Beatrice; he suffers numerous comic indignities during the 'gulling' scene (Act 2 Scene 3) and is cruelly mocked for his lovesick appearance (Act 3 Scene 2). One Benedick tottered on stage in fashionable high-heeled shoes; another Benedick had to endure his friends snatching his new hat, handkerchief, scarf – even his underpants – and throwing them about.

But Benedick becomes more than just a figure of fun when events in the play lead him to a new maturity and rejection of his former comfortable male comradeship. Tricked by his friends into believing Beatrice loves him, he responds whole-heartedly to her desperate unhappiness at Hero's disgrace. His response to her command to 'Kill Claudio' is brave and admirable and his resignation from the prince's service is spoken with manly dignity.

Perhaps his most redeeming feature is his self-awareness, for he is almost always able to laugh at himself. Even when he is finally forced to admit that his earlier stance against marriage was wrong, he does it so whole-heartedly that he turns mockery into respect (Act 5 Scene 4, lines 98–104). In fact, his final admission of his earlier foolishness could almost sum up the whole play: 'for man is a giddy thing, and this is my conclusion'.

◆ Work in pairs as Beatrice and Benedick. It is your tenth wedding anniversary and you are reminiscing. Tell each other why the moment when Beatrice said 'Kill Claudio' was so important to you and how different life would have been if Benedick had chosen differently.

◆ Benedick is paradoxically both serious and comic. List the occasions when he is very much a figure of fun and the times when he acts very much as the 'moral centre' of the play. Write a paragraph giving your views on the part Beatrice plays in provoking him to act as both fool and hero.

◆ Imagine you are preparing to act the part of Benedick. How do you see your journey through the play? Write notes on how you want the audience to perceive you in each of your scenes. Use some of the activities on page 181 to help you find different ways into an understanding of his motives and personality.

This Benedick (left) returned from the war with his head covered in a blood-stained bandage – which he removed, when all the civilians had gone, to reveal no trace of a wound.

'You always end with a jade's trick: I know you of old.' This Benedick, also just back from the war, knew exactly how to annoy Beatrice.

Hero and Claudio: two courtly lovers

Beatrice and Benedick may dominate the play, but the main plot concerns Hero and Claudio, whose love story begins the action and drives all subsequent events. They are a very conventional young couple who happily conform to the accepted rituals of aristocratic Elizabethan courtship and marriage: wooing by proxy, settlement of the dowry, formal betrothal and marriage.

Hero is the typical dutiful and obedient young Elizabethan woman, largely silent and passive in the presence of men. Her name symbolises faithful love (see p. 104). Many modern actresses have found it hard to stomach Hero's passivity, saying they would have told Claudio just where to stick his accusations. However, Shakespeare does give some depth to her character in two intimate all-female scenes (Act 3 Scenes 1 and 4).

Claudio is very much the model Elizabethan lord, courageous in battle and a close friend of the prince. But he is young and inexperienced, which leaves him vulnerable to Don John's plotting. Although Elizabethan audiences may have seen nothing mercenary in his enquiring after Hero's inheritance and would have understood his anger at being foisted with an unchaste bride, modern audiences often find him shallow and insensitive.

Hero is betrothed a second time to a penitent Claudio.

◆ Write character notes on the two lovers. Use some of the activities on page 181 to help you. Consider especially how sympathetic/ unpleasant Claudio should be, and how passive and forgiving Hero should be.

Don John and Don Pedro: two royal brothers

Struggles for power within a royal family were not unusual in Shakespeare's time. A bastard offspring like Don John was a particular threat, because he could challenge the legitimate claims of his brother.

The bastard also threatened the undisputed inheritance of family property, an all-important matter to wealthy Elizabethans. Bastards were therefore regarded as evil and malicious and frequently appeared in the theatre as the stage villain.

Don John is from the start an unsettling presence, virtually silent amidst elegant talkers. He skilfully manipulates Don Pedro, Claudio and Leonato by playing on their fear of the unfaithful wife and the bastard offspring, but is perhaps not too serious a threat to Messina society. He is, for example, quite slow to catch on to Borachio's plan (Act 2 Scene 2) and Shakespeare allows him to fade from the scene once the wedding has been ruined.

Don Pedro is a Spanish prince and ruler of Sicily, who seems assured and confident at the start of the play. During the recent military campaign he has apparently taken Claudio under his wing and continues to do so, but now tutors him in the art of courtship rather than war.

He shares with his half-brother a liking for trickery and plotting, although his deceptions are not maliciously intended. Yet, despite his apparently jovial nature, many productions have him end the play as a rather sad and lonely figure (see picture on p. xii (bottom) in the colour section).

'That one may smile, and smile, and be a villain' (*Hamlet*, Act 1 Scene 5, line 108). Leonato (left) greets Don Pedro (centre) and a smiling Don John (right).

◆ Write three or four paragraphs comparing and contrasting the two royal brothers. Use page 181 (and scene activities like those on pp. 20, 76, 138 and 160) to help you clarify your ideas.

Dogberry, Verges and the Watch

Dogberry and Verges are very much a comic double act. Their function in the play is to discover the plot against Hero, yet be so incompetent that the news is almost never reported to Leonato. The comedy they bring also helps to balance the near-tragic events that surround them.

Dogberry is not merely a comic mangler of words as he attempts to ape the elegant language of the aristocrats. He has a range of moods: grovellingly respectful to Leonato, condescending towards his partner Verges, outraged that he should be called an ass. The naive dignity of his response to this insult is laughable, yet rather touching.

Verges is very much the straight man in the comic partnership and has often been played as a small, ancient man, in contrast to the more robust Dogberry (see picture on p. 96). He is eager to assist and agree with his superior, who promptly puts him down whenever he shows the slightest hint of initiative (Act 3 Scene 5, lines 23–31).

The Town Watch (nightwatchmen) have always been a rich source of comedy. When one Dogberry instructed them to 'call at all the alehouses' (Act 3 Scene 3, line 36), they immediately rushed off stage to do just that and had to be recalled by a blast from his whistle.

Some productions cast professional comedians like Gareth Hale (centre) in the role of Dogberry, just as Shakespeare's company did (see p. 78).

◆ You are to play the part of Dogberry. For each of your scenes write a paragraph giving two or three examples of the comic effects (slapstick, verbal, facial expression, mannerisms, etc.) you want to create. Use some of the activities on page 181 (and scene activities like those on pp. 78, 94, 96, 124 and 144) to help you clarify your ideas.

Activities on characters

a You can build up your understanding of a character by what they say, what other characters say about them, and by their actions. This is helpful not just for understanding the major characters but the lesser characters too. As you follow them through the play:

- Select lines or phrases they speak which you think are typical of them at particular moments.
- Collect examples of what is said by other characters about them.
- Collect examples of their actions (actions, as well as words, reveal what a character is like).

Then try one of the following activities.

Either put together a short scene featuring two or more of the characters you have studied using the methods listed above. Show your characters in as typical a light as possible.

Or make a visual display (e.g. a wall chart, or a coursework folder of illustrations, quotations and your own comments).

Or use the three types of example to help you write an extended essay which analyses a character's 'journey' through the play.

b Explore a character's motives in one of the following ways:

- **'Hot-seating'** One person steps into role as the character. Group members ask questions of the 'why did you do this?' type. For example, Don John could be asked to explain his hostility to Don Pedro and Claudio, to women and to society in general.
- **'Psychiatrist's couch'** One person becomes the character and is psychoanalysed by a partner or small group. For example, Benedick or Claudio could be questioned about their treatment of women.
- **'Chat show'** Your character appears as a celebrity on a television talk show and is questioned by the host.
- **'Autobiography'** Imagine yourself as a character. Write your life story.
- **'Biography'** Step into role as a character and write a biography of another character. For example, Hero writing about her father.

c Collect 'casting photographs' from magazines or newspapers. Cut out and display the ones you think look like characters in the play. Write a caption under each picture saying why you chose it.

d See a production of the play. Afterwards, write about several characters, stating whether each looked and acted as you expected – or did not expect! You will find further ideas to help you with this on page 195.

The language of *Much Ado About Nothing*

People in Messina are always talking. At times their conversation is light, confident, friendly, quick and volatile. At other times it is dark and intense, full of taunts, cold malice, hurt anger, innocent bewilderment, grief and despair, as events force people to confront the painful 'seeming truths' about themselves and those most dear to them.

Shakespeare achieves this through language which is amazingly varied: blank verse, rhyming couplets, quatrains, lyrical songs and, above all, prose that is by turns heavily patterned, elegantly balanced, tauntingly witty, good-naturedly teasing, angry and abusive, precariously rambling, pompously self-important.

Imagery

Much Ado About Nothing is rich in imagery: vivid words and phrases which conjure up emotionally charged mental pictures or associations. Imagery stirs the imagination, deepens dramatic impact and gives insight into character. Certain images recur, most notably images of outward appearance, as when Claudio likens Hero to a 'rotten orange' (Act 4 Scene 1, line 27), evoking a sense of outer beauty and inner corruption. A related image theme which runs through the play is fashion and clothes ('apparel'). In the opening scene, Beatrice declares that Benedick 'wears' his loyalty 'but as the fashion of his hat, it ever changes with the next block [hat shape]'. This theme is explored in more detail on pages 170–3.

Shakespeare's imagery uses metaphor, simile and personification. All are comparisons.

A **simile** compares one thing to another using 'like' or 'as'. Don Pedro, on hearing Borachio confirm Hero's innocence, asks Claudio, 'Runs not this speech like iron through your blood?' Benedick thinks Beatrice would exceed Hero 'as much in beauty as the first of May doth the last of December' – if only she didn't have such a terrible temper!

A **metaphor** is also a comparison, suggesting that two apparently dissimilar things are actually the same. Benedick says of the disappointed Claudio, 'Alas poor hurt fowl, now will he creep into sedges [thick grass]'.

Personification turns things into persons, giving them human feelings or attributes. Beatrice, for example, talks of 'Repentance, . . . with his bad legs' and how a 'star danced' when she was born.

Classical allusions also contribute to the richness of the play's imagery. Educated Elizabethans loved to display their learning and command of language and would certainly have enjoyed the references to Classical mythology as they watched a performance of *Much Ado About Nothing*:

Jove   In Roman mythology Jove was king of the gods. When he travelled the earth in human disguise, Philemon, a poor peasant, gave him hospitality in his humble cottage (see Act 2 Scene 1, lines 69–70). Jove was a habitual adulterer. To keep his sexual liaisons secret from his wife, he adopted many disguises (e.g. bull, satyr, swan), and was thus able to seduce many young women like Europa (see Act 5 Scene 4, lines 43–51) and make them pregnant.

Troilus and Cressida   Troilus loved Cressida faithfully. She swore to be true to him, but proved faithless (see Act 5 Scene 2, line 24).

Hercules   Hercules was the ancient Greek strong-man. He performed many mighty physical tasks (the 'Labours of Hercules', see Act 2 Scene 1, line 275) and numerous sexual ones too, such as impregnating all fifty daughters of the King of Thespis in one night! Cupid later punished him by making him the love-slave of Omphale, queen of Lydia, who beat and ridiculed him, dressing herself in his armour while he was set to do the cooking, spinning and other female tasks (see Act 2 Scene 1, line 191).

♦ Find out which characters make the allusions above. Write down the quotations and alongside each write why they do so (e.g. to impress, amuse, express fear or anger). Afterwards write an explanation of how the references to Jove, Hercules and Troilus and Cressida echo particular themes in the play.

♦ Simile, metaphor, personification and classical allusion are all used one after another during Benedick's account of his traumatic masked dance with Beatrice, 'Oh she misused me . . . perturbation follows her' (Act 2 Scene 1, lines 181–97). Write down the relevant quotations and label them.

Antithesis

Antithesis is the opposition of ideas, words or phrases against each other, as when Beatrice exclaims, 'I had rather hear my dog bark at a crow than a man swear he loves me' (Act 1 Scene 1, lines 97–8). Antithesis expresses conflict (e.g. 'dog bark' stands in contrast to 'man swear') and is especially powerful in *Much Ado About Nothing* with its oppositions between men and women, brother and brother, father and daughter, marriage and independence, truth and lies.

◆ In a play full of deceptions and disguises, appearance is constantly in conflict with reality. Claudio, for example, is convinced he has been an eye-witness to Hero committing an act of infidelity. Turn to Act 4 Scene 1, lines 28–37, 50–55 and 96–101. Write down all the antitheses he uses to express what he believes is Hero's outward purity but inner corruption.

Repetition

Repeated words, phrases, rhythms and sounds add intensity to the moment or episode. Repetitions are at first used elegantly and playfully, as when Benedick jokes with his friends about 'troths and faiths':

DON PEDRO By my troth, I speak my thought.
CLAUDIO And in faith, my lord, I spoke mine.
BENEDICK And by my two faiths and troths, my lord, I spoke mine.

Act 1 Scene 1, lines 166–8

This contrasts sharply with, for example, Leonato's outburst of shame and disappointment at the wedding, where he repeatedly asks questions and repeats 'I', 'thou', 'one', 'she', 'mine'.

◆ Speak Leonato's words (Act 4 Scene 1, lines 114–32), using physical movements to emphasise the repetitions (e.g. pointing, making a gesture, striking your chest).

Lists

Shakespeare seems to have enjoyed 'piling up' words and phrases rather like a list, as in Don Pedro's description of Benedick's multinational fashion sense: like 'a Dutchman today, a Frenchman tomorrow . . . a German from the waist downward . . . and a Spaniard from the hip upward' (Act 3 Scene 2, lines 25–8). A more sombre list is Don John's brooding self-analysis: 'I cannot hide what I am . . .' (Act 1 Scene 3, lines 10–13).

◆ Select a list from the play that you enjoy and work out a way of acting each item. See, as an example, Activity 2 on page 56, which looks at Claudio's over-the-top description of Beatrice's lovesick grief.

Puns and other wordplay

The Elizabethans loved wordplay of all kinds and puns were especially popular. When a word has two or more different meanings, playing on that ambiguity (i.e. punning) can surprise, amuse and sometimes hurt. Nearly everyone in Leonato's household enjoys playing with words, particularly if they have a possible sexual meaning.

Beatrice (Act 2 Scene 1, line 223) says the jealous and resentful Claudio is as 'civil as an orange', punning on the similarities of the two words 'civil' and 'Seville' (a bitter-tasting orange). 'Dies' was a euphemism for sexual orgasm, so when Claudio says that Beatrice 'dies' for love of Benedick (Act 3 Scene 2, lines 50–1) Don Pedro can't resist replying that she will have to be 'buried with her face upwards'.

Sometimes the wordplay bounces back and forth between characters (termed **repartee**). Shakespeare uses this very early on in the play, first between Beatrice and the Messenger to show her sharply barbed wit and then between her and Benedick to set up their bristlingly witty relationship (Act 1 Scene 1, lines 23–70 and 86–107).

In pairs or threes, compile an assignment describing the different uses of puns and other sorts of wordplay in *Much Ado About Nothing*. The following activities will help you clarify your ideas:

- Speak together the following examples of repartee: Act 1 Scene 1, lines 151–215, Act 3 Scene 2, lines 1–54 and Act 5 Scene 4, lines 40–51. Decide how and why the men's repartee changes in tone.
- Read Beatrice and Leonato's conversation (Act 2 Scene 1, lines 1–60) and Margaret and Benedick's (Act 5 Scene 2, lines 1–16). Decide why each woman uses such 'foul language'.
- Read Act 4 Scene 1, lines 265–316 and Act 5 Scene 2, lines 32–79. In what ways is Beatrice and Benedick's wordplay more than merely comic?

Malapropisms

Dogberry's particular talent is for malapropisms (mistakenly using one word for another that sounds similar). Where others in the play deliberately use language to distort and deceive, Dogberry baffles people without realising he is doing so.

- Dogberry's attitude to law enforcement (Act 3 Scene 3, lines 21–60) is the exact opposite to what it should be: go to sleep on duty, keep away from criminals and so on. Look at the malapropisms he uses (see pp. 78, 94 and 120). List the ones that are actual *reversals* of what he should have said.

Shakespeare's prose

The majority of *Much Ado About Nothing* is written in a flexible prose style that changes its qualities with each new character and situation.

But while it may be fluid, Shakespeare's prose is none the less carefully structured in its imagery, rhythms, repetitions, antitheses, lists and wordplay. The result is prose dialogue where the sentences, phrases and words constantly balance, reflect and oppose each other. The following are examples of the variety of effects Shakespeare creates.

Elegant politeness   Leonato, Don Pedro and the Messenger set the tone in the opening scene (see Activity 1, p. 4). Each strives to outdo the other in elegantly balanced compliments and observations (e.g. 'figure of a lamb . . . feats of a lion', Act 1 Scene 1, line 12). Beatrice, of course, refuses to play this game!

Good-natured wit and repartee   Don Pedro, Claudio and Benedick love to demonstrate their friendship in banter and teasing (see Act 1 Scene 1, lines 151–215). When, for example, Don Pedro asks to know what 'secret' his friends were discussing, Benedick playfully gives his 'short' answer: Claudio is in love with 'Leonato's short daughter'.

Rigid single-mindedness   Don John's speech is like a mask. His first words (Act 1 Scene 1, line 116) show an outward politeness, but his inner malice and resentment are revealed in the stiff and heavy sentence patterns of his remarks in Act 1 Scene 3, lines 8–13 and 20–27 (see Activity 1, p. 20). Later, his hatred is concealed behind the apparently concerned manner of his warning to Don Pedro and Claudio (Act 3 Scene 2, lines 59–100).

Attack and counter-attack   The sharpest encounters in the play are between Beatrice and Benedick. What begins apparently playfully (Act 1 Scene 1, lines 86–107) becomes at the masked dance increasingly acrimonious, leaving Benedick wishing he could be anywhere else 'rather than hold three words conference with this Harpy' (Act 2 Scene 1, line 204).

Rambling incoherence   Dogberry's wandering sentences match his rambling brain. He studiously explains why the Watch must have nothing to do with criminals (Act 3 Scene 3, lines 21–50) and fails at great length to tell Leonato vital information that might have averted Hero's public humiliation (Act 3 Scene 5). When he is not botching the cross-examination, he is smarting at being called an ass (Act 4 Scene 2).

Complex and intense dialogue   Much of the prose Beatrice and Benedick speak generates a sense of two very intelligent minds at work.

The way they speak to each other in their initial encounters is aggressive and searching as each probes the other's defences:

> BEATRICE I wonder that you will still be talking, Signor Benedick, nobody marks you.
> BENEDICK What, my dear Lady Disdain! Are you yet living?
>
> *Act 1 Scene 1, lines 86–8*

Yet, beneath the mockery lies a more complex relationship. As the play unfolds, both show a certain insecurity, a fear of either losing the other's respect ('she told me, not thinking I had been myself, that I was the prince's jester', Act 2 Scene 1, lines 183–4) or admitting their own vulnerability ('marry once before he won [my heart] of me, with false dice', Act 2 Scene 1, lines 212–13).

Hero's dishonouring, however, forces them to shed their defensive posture and the prose they speak to each other takes on the complexity and intensity of verse, a subtle and fluctuating meeting of minds. See Activity 1 on page 116 for a way to explore the complex dialogue leading up to and after Beatrice's famous challenge to 'Kill Claudio'.

◆ Find examples of the following kinds of prose in the play and identify language techniques like those outlined in this chapter (simile, metaphor, personification, classical allusions, antithesis, repetition, lists, puns and other wordplay):
  – Young women talking together excitedly and irritably; a young woman flirting and making jokes with sexual undertones.
  – Young men joking uneasily; drunken men speaking cynically; old men speaking disapprovingly to a young woman.
  – A man choosing his words carefully so as not to offend his superior; a man offended by his superior but trying to hide it.
  – A man desperately trying to make sense of his own sudden and overwhelming change of beliefs.

Racist language?

Benedick, Margaret and Claudio refer unflatteringly in the play to Turks, Ethiops (i.e. black-skinned people) and Jews (a grudgingly tolerated minority in Shakespeare's England, often subject to verbal abuse). Read their words and the context in which they say them (Act 2 Scene 3, line 212, Act 3 Scene 4, line 42, and Act 5 Scene 4, line 38). Do you find their remarks offensive and accuse Shakespeare of racism, or would you defend him? Write a paragraph giving reasons for your point of view.

Shakespeare's blank verse

Although only one third of the play is written in blank (unrhymed) verse, it is spoken at significant moments and with powerful effect (see p. 189). There is nothing difficult about Shakespeare's blank verse. Many believe it is based very closely on the natural rhythms of English speech. Each line is an **iambic pentameter**. In Greek, *penta* means five and an *iamb* is a 'foot' of two syllables, the first unstressed (×) and the second stressed (/). So an iambic pentameter is five sets of unstressed + stressed syllables (often expressed as 'de-DUM, de-DUM, de-DUM, de-DUM, de-DUM'). The first verse line of the play is a good example:

×　　/　　×　　/　×　　/　×　　/ ×　　/

My liege, your highness now may do me good.

Act 1 Scene 1, line 216

This rhythmic pattern and energy is frequently varied (but never completely lost), so that many different effects are created. Sometimes a line is shaped into two halves with a mid-line pause (**caesura**) and an end-of-line pause (**end-stopping**). Very often one line will 'flow' into the next (**enjambement** or **run-on line**). Read the following examples aloud to hear some of these differences:

- Claudio's farewell to Hero (Act 4 Scene 1, lines 93–101)
- Leonato's grief (Act 4 Scene 1, lines 129–36)
- The Friar's plan (Act 4 Scene 1, lines 203–36).

Couplets, quatrains and sonnets

Shakespeare occasionally uses rhymed verse in *Much Ado About Nothing* to heighten theatrical effect, to deepen the emotional and imaginative power of a scene or to create a sense of closure.

- ◆ The sad exit of Hero and her family (Act 4 Scene 1, lines 244–7) is marked by four rhyming lines (ABAB) called a **quatrain**. Practise speaking the Friar's lines as solemnly as you can.
- ◆ Don Pedro and Claudio speak quatrains at the conclusion of the memorial tribute to Hero (Act 5 Scene 3, lines 24–7 and 30–3). What effect do these lines create?
- ◆ Why does Shakespeare have Hero speak a **couplet** (two rhyming lines) as she exits at Act 3 Scene 1, lines 105–6?

Everyone laughs when Beatrice and Benedick's sonnets are produced at the end of the play. Many Elizabethan love sonnets had a rhyme scheme of three quatrains (ABAB/CDCD/EFEF) and a final couplet (GG). See Activity 2 on page 70.

Songs

Shakespeare was well aware of the power of music and song to enhance dramatic effect. Balthasar's song 'Sigh no more, ladies' (Act 2 Scene 3, lines 53–68), for example, is placed at one of the turning points in the Beatrice–Benedick plot to sound a mocking echo to the play's theme of deception and 'The fraud of men'. Despite Don Pedro and Benedick's comments, this song has often been movingly sung (see Activity 1, p. 52).

Benedick's song, 'The God of love' (Act 5 Scene 2, lines 18–22) is undoubtedly badly sung, as even Benedick has to admit. The song was very popular in Shakespeare's time and much imitated, so the comedy of Benedick as melancholy lover would have been immediately apparent (see Activity 2, p. 146).

◆ Few people have been impressed with the words of the funeral song, 'Pardon, goddess of the night' (Act 5 Scene 3, lines 12–21). Write director's notes on how this might be effectively staged using costume, scenic effects, movement, vocal effects, music, sound, lighting and so on.

Why does Shakespeare switch between verse and prose?

An Elizabethan audience would have expected high-status characters to speak verse, particularly in scenes of high drama or emotional intensity. Prose was the traditional mode of expression for low-status characters in more relaxed comic scenes. Dogberry, for example, always speaks in prose. Shakespeare, however, bends the rules in subtly dramatic ways.

The intelligent and worldly-wise Beatrice and Benedick prefer prose. High-status characters like Leonato, Claudio and Don Pedro will speak an elegant and witty prose when relaxed, but at more intense moments readily switch to verse. Claudio, for example, leads Don Pedro into verse to talk of his love for Hero (Act 1 Scene 1, line 216).

◆ Find the moments when even Beatrice and Benedick speak in verse. Decide what has prompted them to do so.

◆ The men speak largely in prose when tricking Benedick (Act 2 Scene 3). The women speak entirely in verse when tricking Beatrice (Act 3 Scene 1). Suggest three possible reasons for the difference.

◆ Look at the transitions between verse and prose in Act 4 Scene 1 and Act 5 Scene 1. At each transition write down the particular change of mood that is being signalled. For example, Don Pedro and Claudio switch from joking prose to serious verse when they learn to their horror that Hero was innocent of any misconduct (Act 5 Scene 1, lines 214–21).

Much Ado About Nothing in performance

Much Ado About Nothing at the Globe

Because women were banned from acting in public in Shakespeare's day, Beatrice, Hero, Margaret and other female parts were played by boys. There were no elaborate sets on the bare stage of the Globe Theatre. Only a few props were used (swords, chairs, etc.) but the actors wore attractive and expensive costumes, usually the fashionable dress of the times. Comments by Borachio and others in the play about 'that deformed thief fashion' would have been appreciated by Shakespeare's audience.

The reconstructed Globe Theatre is on London's Bankside, close to the site on which Shakespeare's Globe once stood. Many of the productions here are staged as Shakespeare's audiences probably saw them. In an intriguing reversal of Elizabethan practice, the 2004 production of *Much Ado About Nothing* (above and opposite) was performed with an all-female cast.

What this production inevitably lacked in sexual tension, it made up for in speed and pace. There was a ferocious interpretation of Beatrice and a well-padded Benedick, who lent weight to Beatrice's barbed comments about his 'excellent stomach' (Act 1 Scene 1, line 38).

190

An angry and formidable
Beatrice (Globe Theatre, 2004).

A likeably swaggering Benedick,
dressed in the baggiest of breeches
(Globe Theatre, 2004).

◆ If you were directing an all–male or all-female version of *Much Ado
About Nothing*, what special qualities could such a cast bring to the
play?

Eighteenth- and nineteenth-century stagings of *Much Ado About Nothing*

In the eighteenth century, David Garrick's productions of the play were swift, lively and entertaining, with Beatrice and Benedick the dominant interest. Costumed in fashionable dress of the day, Garrick and his leading ladies played the 'merry war' as an aggressively vigorous battle for supremacy.

Nineteenth-century productions paid more attention to visual effect, with rich Elizabethan-style costumes and elaborate scene changes which slowed the pace of performances considerably. The dominant mood was of romantic happiness with little emphasis on the darker elements of the play. The most admired Beatrices of this period were those who softened her aggressive energy and conformed more to the Victorian stereotype of ideal womanhood: sweet, gentle and delicate.

A drawing of the church scene (Act 4 Scene 1) from Henry Irving's 1882 production. It was particularly praised for its 'splendour of spectacle' and 'minute attention to detail'. How many named characters can you identify?

Modern productions

Modern productions have employed a huge variety of ways of staging *Much Ado About Nothing*. But nearly all use a single basic set which can be quickly adapted to allow the play to flow swiftly from scene to scene. Such sets avoid lengthy breaks for scene shifting. Although often given an Elizabethan setting (see pp. 132 and 142), the play has been placed in many other communities and historical periods: Restoration England, nineteenth-century British India (below), a Middle American town in the 1890s, a 1930s cruise ship, Second World War England.

In the second half of the twentieth century, the rise of feminism saw a shift away from sweet and romantic Beatrices to more independent interpretations as well as a more jaundiced view of marriage. One production heavily emphasised Hero's mistreatment and played Claudio in a more than usually unlikeable fashion. The traditional happy ending was chillingly questioned – everyone was dressed in black.

The 1976 Royal Shakespeare Company production was set in nineteenth-century British India. While some felt this effectively highlighted the social divide between rulers and subjects in the play, others were uneasy about its racial overtones. Put the case for both points of view.

Set in mid twentieth-century Sicily, this 2002 Royal Shakespeare Company production cast Benedick as a military bachelor-soldier who looked 'like an ageing walrus' and a Beatrice who was so angry at the men's treatment of Hero that she kicked over the church pews.

This 1988 Royal Shakespeare Company production chose a formidably Amazonian Beatrice, seen here in the dance scene grabbing a diminutive, balding Benedick, whom she proceeded to swing across her back and throw about.

194

Stage your own production of *Much Ado About Nothing*

Talk together about the period and place in which you will set your play: somewhere where wealth and social class, fashion and costume, male and female codes of honour and duty are important? Then choose one or more of the following activities. Your finished assignment can be a file of drawings, notes and suggestions, a live presentation of your ideas (e.g. a talk) or an actual performance.

- ◆ Design the set – how can it be used for particular scenes?
- ◆ Design the costumes (a significant element in this play!) – look at past examples, but invent your own.
- ◆ Design the props – furnishings and hand props (masks, swords, etc.).
- ◆ Design a lighting and sound programme – for one or two scenes.
- ◆ Design the publicity poster – make people want to see your play!
- ◆ Design a 'flyer' – a small handbill to advertise the production.
- ◆ Design the programme – think about layout, content, number of pages.
- ◆ Write character notes for actors' guidance.
- ◆ Work out a five-minute presentation to show to potential sponsors.

Visit a production of *Much Ado About Nothing*

Shakespeare wrote *Much Ado About Nothing* to be acted, watched and enjoyed, not to be studied for examinations! So see a live performance. Prepare for a school or college visit using the following:

- ◆ Everyone chooses a character (or an incident or scene) to watch especially closely. Write down your expectations before you go. Report back to the class on how your expectations for 'your' character were fulfilled or challenged.
- ◆ Choose your favourite line in the play. Listen carefully to how it is spoken. Does it add to your understanding?
- ◆ Your teacher will probably be able to provide one or two published reviews of the production. Talk together about whether you should read the reviews before or after you see the play for yourself. After the visit, discuss how far you agree or disagree with the reviews.
- ◆ Write your own review. Record your own perceptions of what you actually saw and heard – and your feelings about the production.

Finally, remember two points:

- • Preparation is always valuable, but too much preparation can kill the enjoyment of a theatre visit.
- • Every production is different. There is no such thing as a single right way to 'do' Shakespeare. But you might think that there are 'wrong' ways!

William Shakespeare
1564–1616

1564 Born Stratford-upon-Avon, eldest son of John and Mary Shakespeare.

1582 Marries Anne Hathaway of Shottery, near Stratford.

1583 Daughter, Susanna, born.

1585 Twins, son and daughter, Hamnet and Judith, born.

1592 First mention of Shakespeare in London. Robert Greene, another playwright, described Shakespeare as 'an upstart crow beautified with our feathers . . .'. Greene seems to have been jealous of Shakespeare. He mocked Shakespeare's name, calling him 'the only Shake-scene in a country' (presumably because Shakespeare was writing successful plays).

1595 A shareholder in The Lord Chamberlain's Men, an acting company that became extremely popular.

1596 Son Hamnet dies, aged 11.
Father, John, granted arms (acknowledged as a gentleman).

1597 Buys New Place, the grandest house in Stratford.

1598 Acts in Ben Jonson's *Every Man in His Humour*.

1599 Globe Theatre opens on Bankside. Performances in the open air.

1601 Father, John, dies.

1603 James I grants Shakespeare's company a royal patent: The Lord Chamberlain's Men become The King's Men and play about twelve performances each year at court.

1607 Daughter, Susanna, marries Dr John Hall.

1608 Mother, Mary, dies.

1609 The King's Men begin performing indoors at Blackfriars Theatre.

1610 Probably returns from London to live in Stratford.

1616 Daughter, Judith, marries Thomas Quiney.
Dies. Buried in Holy Trinity Church, Stratford-upon-Avon.

The plays and poems
(no one knows exactly when he wrote each play)

1589–95 *The Two Gentlemen of Verona, The Taming of the Shrew, First, Second and Third Parts of King Henry VI, Titus Andronicus, King Richard III, The Comedy of Errors, Love's Labour's Lost, A Midsummer Night's Dream, Romeo and Juliet, King Richard II* (and the long poems *Venus and Adonis* and *The Rape of Lucrece*).

1596–9 *King John, The Merchant of Venice, First and Second Parts of King Henry IV, The Merry Wives of Windsor, Much Ado About Nothing, King Henry V, Julius Caesar* (and probably the *Sonnets*).

1600–5 *As You Like It, Hamlet, Twelfth Night, Troilus and Cressida, Measure for Measure, Othello, All's Well That Ends Well, Timon of Athens, King Lear.*

1606–11 *Macbeth, Antony and Cleopatra, Pericles, Coriolanus, The Winter's Tale, Cymbeline, The Tempest.*

1613 *King Henry VIII, The Two Noble Kinsmen* (both probably with John Fletcher).

1623 Shakespeare's plays published as a collection (now called the First Folio).